Teacher's Resource Book 4

with Online Audio

Second Edition

Kathryn Escribano with Caroline Nixon & Michael Tomlinson

CAMBRIDGE
UNIVERSITY PRESS

CAMBRIDGE
UNIVERSITY PRESS

University Printing House, Cambridge CB2 8BS, United Kingdom

One Liberty Plaza, 20th Floor, New York, NY 10006, USA

477 Williamstown Road, Port Melbourne, VIC 3207, Australia

4843/24, 2nd Floor, Ansari Road, Daryaganj, Delhi – 110002, India

79 Anson Road, #06–04/06, Singapore 079906

Cambridge University Press is part of the University of Cambridge.

It furthers the University's mission by disseminating knowledge in the pursuit of education, learning and research at the highest international levels of excellence.

www.cambridge.org
Information on this title: www.cambridge.org/9781107658493

First published 2009
Second edition 2015
Reprinted 2017

Printed in Italy by Rotolito Lombarda S.p.A.

A catalogue record for this publication is available from the British Library

ISBN 978-1-107-65849-3 Teacher's Resource Book with Online Audio 4
ISBN 978-1-107-65685-7 Pupil's Book 4
ISBN 978-1-107-66146-2 Activity Book with Online Resources 4
ISBN 978-1-107-62905-9 Teacher's Book 4
ISBN 978-1-107-66711-2 Class Audio CDs 4 (3 CDs)
ISBN 978-1-107-66611-5 Flashcards 4 (Book of 103)
ISBN 978-1-107-65564-5 Interactive DVD with Teacher's Booklet 4
ISBN 978-1-107-43244-4 Presentation Plus 4
ISBN 978-1-107-65461-7 Language Portfolio 4
ISBN 978-1-107-67281-9 Posters 4
ISBN 978-1-107-61806-0 Tests CD-ROM and Audio CD 3–4

Additional resources for this publication at www.cambridge.org/kidsbox

Contents

Introduction

- This Teacher's Resource Book is designed to help you and your pupils make the most of *Kid's Box 4* as well as providing practice for the Cambridge English: Young Learners (YLE) Tests. There are three main sections in this Book:
  - Worksheets
  - Word cards
  - Practice tests

Worksheets

- There are two reinforcement worksheets and two extension worksheets per unit. The former are designed for revision and to help those pupils who need extra practice while the latter are designed to cater for the needs of fast finishers. However, these worksheets not only provide a resource for mixed-ability classes, but also offer material to set as homework or for the rest of the class to use while you work individually with a pupil on a speaking test.

- Reinforcement worksheet 1 for each unit focuses on key vocabulary, while reinforcement worksheet 2 provides further practice of the structures. Extension worksheet 1 is more challenging. It is designed for fast finishers who need a more cognitively demanding type of activity. Extension worksheet 2 offers further exploitation of the unit story.

- There is also a song worksheet for each unit. These always give the song lyrics and a song-based activity which varies from unit to unit. These worksheets are best done once pupils are familiar with the song. The songs are provided online on the *Kid's Box* website, but you can also use the Class Audio CDs. Please note that the track numbers refer to *Kid's Box 4 Online Audio*.

- Finally, each unit has a content-based topic worksheet. As explained in the Teacher's Book, the content-based lessons in the Pupil's Book and Activity Book aim to teach and reinforce understanding of subject topics which pupils learn in their other classes, through the medium of English. Thus, there is a dual aim: that of learning subject content and learning language. The topic worksheets in this Resource Book add to, and go beyond, the content-based pages in the Pupil's Book and Activity Book.

- There is a page of teaching notes before the worksheets for each unit. These notes include optional follow-up activities which encourage interaction between pupils and add a useful dimension to the worksheet. You may find that one type of follow-up activity works better than another with your particular class, in which case you can use the suggestions as a springboard for adapting other worksheets.

- You may find, according to the particular interests of a pupil, that in one unit, he/she needs a reinforcement worksheet while in other units, or at other times, the same pupil can more profitably do an extension worksheet. Fast finishers may want/need to do reinforcement and extension worksheets.

- You can also use the worksheets as gap-fillers or alternative activities when, for example, some other activity has interfered with the normal running of the class.

- The worksheets can also be used as models for you or your pupils to develop further practice activities. Creating exercises is an excellent way for pupils to consolidate their learning and they will enjoy swapping them with their friends.

- You may find it useful to keep a record of the worksheets each pupil has completed.

- After the resources for each unit, there are two worksheets for each of the following festivals:
  - Halloween
  - Christmas
  - Easter

- The teaching notes for this section contain cultural notes on the festivals which you can use to introduce the topics to the class.

Word cards

- For each unit, there are photocopiable word cards with the key vocabulary items of each unit. These are to support you in the consolidation of literacy in English in the classroom. You may wish to mount the photocopied words on card and laminate them so that they can be used over and over again. You may also like to enlarge them on a photocopier before doing so.

- Some ideas for using the word cards:
  - Display them in the classroom so that the 'walls talk'.
  - Give photocopies to the pupils to make into dictionaries.
  - Use them for rhyme practice, asking pupils to select two that sound the same or one that has the same sound as the word you say.
  - Reveal one letter at a time, asking pupils to spell out the word or guess it.
  - Make them into card games.
  - Use them as prompts when asking pupils to write and speak.

- It is easy to put away one set of word cards as you move on to a new unit, but remember that it is very useful to mix them in with subsequent vocabulary sets. You can use them to recycle and test vocabulary throughout the year.

Practice tests

- There are two progress tests, each covering four units. The tests are suitable for all classes as they review the vocabulary and structures of the preceding units. In addition, they offer specific practice for the Movers level of the Cambridge English: Young Learners (YLE) Tests. The more familiar the pupils are with the various activity types and the test format, the more confidence they will have when they do the YLE Movers Test having completed *Kid's Box 4*.

YLE activity types in *Kid's Box 4* tests

Task	Approximate duration	Expected response	Tips
Listening	25 minutes		Ensure pupils know that each listening text is heard twice. Encourage them to listen to the complete recording before answering questions.
Listen and draw lines.		Draw lines to match names to people in a picture.	Ensure that pupils realise there is one extra name at the top or bottom of the page which will not be mentioned. Make sure the pupils know which first names are male and which are female and which can be both: *Alex, Kim, Pat* and *Sam*. Use the Name cards on page 142. Warn them not to jump to conclusions. They must listen to all the information.
Listen and write.		Write words or numbers in gaps.	Practise by doing similar productive tasks in the classroom. Encourage pupils to be as accurate as possible in their spelling, though some misspellings will be allowed for words not spelt out on the recording. Ensure that pupils realise they have to write responses which make sense, given the prompts.
Listen and draw a line from the day to the correct picture.		Draw lines from days of the week to correct pictures.	Encourage pupils to draw a line to the appropriate picture in the most direct way possible. Make sure they know each day is only used once and one day will not be used at all. Encourage pupils not to leave questions unanswered. Once they have used the days they are sure about, they should make an intelligent guess about the remaining pictures.
Listen and tick the box.		Tick boxes under correct pictures.	Ensure that the pupils listen to the whole dialogue before deciding on their answer. Recycle the exam vocabulary constantly.
Listen and colour and draw or write.		Carry out instructions to colour and draw or write.	Practise colour vocabulary (black, blue, brown, green, grey, orange, pink, purple, red, yellow). Remind pupils that they will either have to draw or write something for one of the questions. Train pupils to listen carefully for prepositional phrases which describe exactly where something is.

Task	Approximate duration	Expected response	Tips
Reading & Writing	30 minutes		**Correct spelling is required in all parts of the Reading & Writing Test.** Encourage pupils to write clearly. It is often better not to use joined-up writing. Train pupils to write only as much as they need to. Give time limits when doing classroom tasks, to help pupils learn time management. Make sure pupils are familiar with the structures and words in the Starters and Movers syllabuses.
Look and read. Choose the correct words and write them on the lines.		Copy correct words next to definitions.	Give pupils practice in reading and writing definitions. Give pupils practice in accurate copying. Remind pupils to copy the whole option and not to add anything extra. Train pupils to correct their spelling.
Look and read. Write 'yes' or 'no'.		Write 'yes' or 'no'.	Give pupils practice in matching sentences to pictures. Remind pupils that the sentence must be completely true according to the picture for a 'yes' answer.
Read the text and choose the best answer.		Choose the correct response by circling a letter.	Remind pupils to read all the options before choosing the correct one. Practise appropriate responses, not just to questions, but also to statements. Give practice with the use of set expressions and with short 'yes'/'no' answers. Give practice with multiple-choice questions.
Read the story. Write one-word answers.		Choose and copy missing words correctly. Tick a box to choose the best title for the story.	Encourage pupils to read holistically for a sense of the text before trying to fill the first gap. Train pupils to read the text surrounding the question to be able to fill the gap correctly. Give practice in guessing which word could go into a gap. Practise choosing the right form of words within sentences and texts. Help pupils to identify words or structures that indicate what form of word the answer should be.
Look at the pictures and read the story. Complete the sentences.		Complete sentences about a story by writing 1, 2 or 3 words.	**Pupils must not write more than three words.** Train pupils to predict an outline of the story from the three pictures and the title. Practise reading for gist. Practise understanding whole texts by selecting titles for paragraphs or complete stories. Practise finding synonyms for nouns, identifying what is being referred to in a text, using pronouns to replace nouns and turning sentences around without altering the meaning. Ensure that the words chosen to complete the sentences are grammatically correct.
Read the text. Choose the right words and write them on the lines.		Complete a text by selecting the correct words and copying them in the corresponding gaps.	Practise choosing and forming the correct type of word to fit into sentences and texts. Remind pupils to choose from the three options given. Practise general reading skills.

Task	Approximate duration	Expected response	Tips
Speaking	5–7 minutes		The mark is based on ratings for interactive listening ability, production of extended responses and pronunciation. Pupils are required to follow simple instructions and talk about different pictures, and to answer simple questions about themselves.
Describe two pictures by using short responses.		Identify four differences between pictures.	Give pupils practice in describing differences between two similar pictures.
Understand the beginning of a story and then continue it based on a series of pictures.		Describe each picture in turn.	Give pupils practice in telling simple picture stories. Practise using *There is/are*, the present tense of the verbs *be* and *have (got)*, the modals *can/can't* and *must/mustn't* and the present continuous.
Suggest a picture which is different and explain why.		Identify the odd one out and give a reason.	Practise identifying the different one in a set of four pictures.
Understand and respond to personal questions.		Answer personal questions.	Give the pupils practice in answering questions about themselves, their families and friends, their homes, their school and free-time activities, their likes and dislikes. Use English to give everyday classroom instructions. Make sure pupils are happy using *Hello, Goodbye* and *Thank you*, and that they have plenty of practice using *Sorry*, or *I don't understand*.

Teacher's notes

Reinforcement worksheet 1

- Pupils count forwards and backwards along the alphabet to find the words. They transfer the information to the form below and complete it about a favourite singer, sports personality or other famous person. Pre-teach/Check the meaning of *job*. The pupils stick a picture of the person into the frame

Key: 2 age, 3 job, 4 hair, 5 wears, 6 likes, 7 can.

- *Optional follow-up activity:* Pupils take it in turns to read the information about their chosen personality (omitting the name and not showing the picture).
The first pupil who guesses who it is gets a point. The winner is the pupil with the most points.

Reinforcement worksheet 2

- Pupils find and circle the job word, as in the model, and then use the words in the crossword to write a description of the teacher. They draw a picture to match the description.

Key: pupils circle *teacher* in the crossword.
Descriptions may vary slightly. A possible answer is *The teacher's got straight black hair. She's wearing a skirt and glasses. She's happy.*

- *Optional follow-up activity:* Pupils write another similar description and swap it with a friend. They draw a picture to match their friend's text.

Extension worksheet 1

- Pupils read the text about Aunt May on page 6 of the Pupil's Book and use the information to choose the right answers. They then read the text about Uncle Fred and prepare a similar multiple-choice quiz.

Key: 2 A, 3 B, 4 C.

- *Optional follow-up activity:* After you have checked the pupils' work, they swap quizzes and answer them.

Extension worksheet 2

- This can be done as a listening exercise (Track 2) or a reading exercise. If you use the audio recording, pause after each frame while the pupils write. Pupils insert the missing vowels. Ask them to count the number of times they have written each letter to see which vowel appears most often in the text. Use the activity to show the children that e is the most common vowel in English and remind them that this is useful for playing *Hangman*. (Generally, exclamations such as *Ooohooo!* and proper names do not count towards vowel frequency because they are not found in dictionaries, but in this activity it is easier if the children count everything.)

Key: See Pupil's Book, page 9.
A 28, E 71, I 42, O 40, U 12.

- *Optional follow-up activity:* Give pupils two minutes to write as many words as possible beginning with e. The winner is the pupil with the most words.

Song worksheet

- Pupils colour the pictures to remind themselves of the sounds in these words. They then look at the underlined parts of the words in the box and decide which colour they rhyme with. They colour them accordingly and then complete the song with the words, using the colour words to guide them. They listen to the song (Track 3) to check their answers.

Key: See Pupil's Book, page 7.

- *Optional follow-up activity:* Ask pupils to find words which rhyme with *brown*, *green* and *red*.

Topic worksheet

- Pupils read about time zones. They count backwards and forwards to draw the times on all the clocks to show what time it is in four other world cities when the boy is doing these four different activities. They use the times on the clocks to help them complete the sentences.

Key: 2 is having lunch, 3 is watching TV, 4 is going to bed.

- *Optional follow-up activity:* Pupils think of five activities that they do in a day and decide what children in the other cities on the worksheet would be doing at that time.

Hello there! Reinforcement worksheet 1

⭐ **Find the words.**

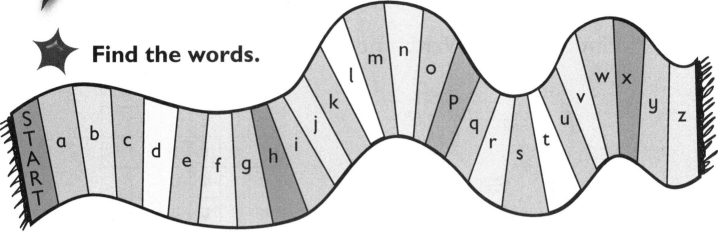

1 Count 14 from the start. Go back 13. Go forward 12.

Go back 8. <u>n</u> <u>a</u> <u>m</u> <u>e</u>

2 Count 1 from the start. Go forward 6. Go back 2. _ _ _

3 Count 10 from the start. Go forward 5. Go back 13. _ _ _

4 Count 8 from the start. Go back 7. Go forward 8.

Go forward 9. _ _ _ _

5 Count 23 from the start. Go back 18. Go back 4. Go forward 17.

Go forward 1. _ _ _ _ _

6 Count 12 from the start. Go back 3. Go forward 2. Go back 6.

Go forward 14. _ _ _ _ _

7 Count 3 from the start. Go back 2. Go forward 13. _ _ _

⭐ **Complete the table. Write about someone famous.**

1 Name		
2		
3		
4		
5		
6		
7		

Hello there! Reinforcement worksheet 2

 Find the jobs. Write and draw.

			c	
h	t		w	u
f	a	r	m	e	r
u	i	o	o	a	l
n	r	u	u	r	y
n		s	s	i	
y		e	t	n	
		r		g	
		s	c		
			h		
			e		

1 <u>The farmer's got curly hair</u>
<u>and a moustache. He's wearing</u>
<u>trousers. He's funny.</u>

					g	
s					l	
k		s	b		a	h
i		t	l		s	a
r	w	r	a		s	i
t	e	a	c	h	e	r
	a	i	k	a	s	
	r	g		p		
	i	h		p		
	n	t		y		
	g					

2 _____

_____

_____

_____

Kid's Box Teacher's Resource Book 4   © Cambridge University Press 2015   **PHOTOCOPIABLE**

Hello there! Extension worksheet 1

 Read the text about Aunt May on page 6 of the Pupil's Book. Choose the right answer.

1 Is Aunt May a doctor?

(A) Yes, she is.

B No, she isn't.

C Yes, she has.

2 Does she work in a little hospital?

A No, she doesn't.

B No, she isn't.

C Yes, she does.

3 Does she always work at night?

A Yes, she does.

B No, she doesn't.

C Yes, she is.

4 Does she like listening to music?

A Yes, she is.

B No, she doesn't.

C Yes, she does.

 Read the text about Uncle Fred on page 6 of the Pupil's Book. Write questions. Ask your friend.

1 _____

_____ ?

A No, he hasn't.

B Yes, he is.

C No, he isn't.

2 _____

_____ ?

A No, he doesn't.

B Yes, he does.

C Yes, he is.

3 _____

_____ ?

A Yes, he has.

B No, he hasn't.

C No, he doesn't.

4 _____

_____ ?

A Yes, he does.

B Yes, he has.

C No, he doesn't.

Extension worksheet 2

Complete the story.

O o o h o o o !
Mr L__ck! Th__s __s
my s__st__r's s__n,
P_t_r. H__ n___ds
Y___r h_lp.

H__ll_,
P__t__r.
W__ll, __
d__n't ...

N__ pr__bl__m,
P__t__r. Wh__t's
th__ m__tt__r?

W__ll, th__r__'s
__ p__cn__c
th__ f __n
B__k__r's P__rk.

B__h! __
p__cn__c
th___f ...

L__t's g__
__nd s___!

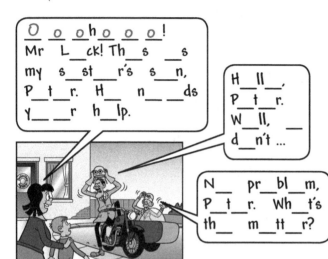

R__ght h__r__, n__xt t__ th__
l__k__. __v__ry t__m__ __ pl__y
w__th my fr___nds s__m__b__dy
t__k__s ___r p__cn__c.

G__ __nd pl__y,
P__t__r. P__t
Y__r f__d
__n th__
bl__nk__t. __'t's
s__f__ w__th __s.

__xc__s__ m__,
s__r. Wh__t c__n
y___ t__ll m__
__b__t th__
p__cn__c th___f?

Y___h,
wh__r__ w__r__
y___ __t
th__s t__m__
y__st__rd__y?

____ ___h! __
w__s __t __
p__cn__c. H__r__
__n th__ p__rk.

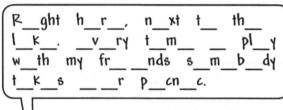

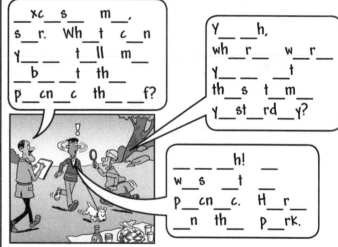

__h__! S__, y__ __
l__k__ p__cn__cs.

__t's __K, P__t__r. __'v__ g__t
y___r p__cn__c.

L__ck, __'v__
g__t th__
p__cn__c
th___f ... __r,
__r, __t's g__t
m__! H__lp!

__h, __r,
th__nk y___,
Mr K__y.

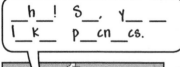

Hello there! # Song worksheet

 ## Colour the pictures.

blue shoe   grey train   yellow boat   white kite

 ## Colour the words.

clothes	Goodbye	shoes	to	Wake	So	to	go	I'm
Goodbye	wake	lose	routine	No	to	day	time
Comb	to	time	~~do~~	My	same	to	You	say

 3 ## Read and write. Listen and check. Sing.

The morning rap,

We [blue] .... do ... it every [grey] ....

The [grey] .... [blue] .... ,

Now listen and [grey] ....

It's seven o'clock,

[grey] .... up, [grey] .... up!

[blue] .... must get up

And have a wash.

Come on, come on,

It's [white] .... [blue] ....

[yellow] ....

Get dressed, get dressed!

Put on your [yellow] ....

Run [blue] .... the kitchen,

Sit on a chair.

Eat your breakfast,

[yellow] .... your hair.

The morning rap …

Clean your teeth.

[yellow] .... [white] ....

[blue] .... [blue] ....

Get your bag,

Put on your [blue] ....

[white] .... [blue] .... Mum,

[white] .... [blue] .... Dad.

[white] .... friends are at school,

[yellow] .... [white] .... not sad.

The morning rap. The morning rap.

Hello there! Topic worksheet

 Read about time zones.

What time is it now? Do you know that it's a different time in different countries? When it's twelve o'clock in the afternoon in England, it's twelve o'clock at night in Australia. The world has different time zones and in some countries there are different time zones. Are there different time zones in your country?

 Draw the times on the clocks.

New York –5	Brasilia –3	London	Athens +2	Tokyo +9

 Complete the sentences.

1 When it's six o'clock in the morning in Brasilia, Bob <u>is starting school.</u>

2 When it's ten o'clock in the evening in Tokyo, Bob _____ .

3 When it's two o'clock in the afternoon in New York, Bob _____
_____ .

4 When it's eleven o'clock at night in Athens, Bob _____
_____ .

Reinforcement worksheet 1

- Pupils discuss Braille and use the key to solve the crossword. They note their answers in the table.

Key: Braille is a language for the blind invented by a Frenchman called Braille. The dots represent the bumps that the blind can feel and 'read' with their fingers.

1 difficult, 2 easy, 3 boring, 4 careful, 5 quick, 6 busy, 7 slow, 8 exciting.

- *Optional follow-up activity:* In pairs or small groups, pupils write sentences, or find them in their Pupil's Book, to act as clues for the crossword. Give them this example for the word *difficult:*

1 *We like his lessons because they're not* _____ . (from Pupil's Book, page 11)

Reinforcement worksheet 2

- Pupils look at the three pictures and choose which one they prefer. They complete and write the sentences. Write this key on the board:
a = 3 b = 2 c = 1

The pupils add up the points to discover what sort of person they are, based on the following key which you can read out to the class:

7–9 points
You are happy doing exciting things. You like difficult activities. You like doing quick things and being busy. You think slow activities are a bit boring.

4–6 points
You like some exciting things but you like activities that are not too difficult. You like some quick activities but you don't need everything to be quick. Sometimes you like to be busy – but not too busy!

3 points
You don't like difficult activities. You like doing slow activities and you are happy when people are quiet. You don't like being busy all the time.

- *Optional follow-up activity:* Pupils think of another school subject involving three alternative activities. They choose their favourite of the three. In groups, they compare their results to produce a survey about favourite activities in different subjects.

Extension worksheet 1

- Pupils read the sentences in the grid. They find the people in the picture and number the boxes accordingly. They then work out the missing numbers by getting each side of the grid to add up to 20. They write *This is the ...* sentences for the other four squares in the grid.

Key: Top line: 1, 4, 5, 10; Middle line: 11, 7; Bottom line: 8, 0, 9, 3.

- *Optional follow-up activity:* Pupils colour in the scene and then write alternative *This is the ...* sentences in their notebooks, for example *This is the boy who is wearing a blue jumper.*

Extension worksheet 2

- Pupils listen to the story (Track 4) and follow on the worksheet. They then follow the instructions to write the sentences from the story. They can write in their notebooks or on the back of the worksheet, as you prefer.

- *Optional follow-up activity:* In groups of four, each pupil cuts out the six frames. The dealer shuffles them and deals them all out. Pupil A puts one of the frames face up on the table and the others race to put down the next frame. The first to do so keeps the cards and play passes to Pupil B, and so on. The game continues until one pupil has won all the cards. Tell the pupils that, in this game, frame 1 follows on from frame 6.

Song worksheet

- Pupils match the rhyming pairs, then complete the song. They listen to the song (Track 5) to check their answers.

Key: See Pupil's Book, page 13.

- *Optional follow-up activity:* In groups, pupils think of as many words as possible to rhyme with the words they have paired.

Topic worksheet

- Pre-teach words you think the pupils may find difficult. Pupils read the text and do the activities. They may need time to measure people at home if they have already measured their friends in class.

Key: 2 65 cm, 3 37.5 cm, 4 42.5 cm.

- *Optional follow-up activity:* Pupils convert the measurements of their classroom objects from page 17 of the Pupil's Book into inches.

Reinforcement worksheet 1

 The crossword is in Braille. What is Braille?

A	B	C	D	E	F	G	H	I	J	K	L	M

N	O	P	Q	R	S	T	U	V	W	X	Y	Z

 Use the Braille key to solve the crossword.

1	di
2	
3	
4	
5	
6	
7	
8	

Crossword answers (vertical): T E R R I B L E

Kid's Box Teacher's Resource Book 4   © Cambridge University Press 2015

Reinforcement worksheet 2

 What do you prefer? Choose a picture.

1 In the playground

playing basketball	skipping	sitting down and talking

I prefer the children who are _____ . Picture ☐

2 In Art lessons

painting	colouring in	learning about art

_____ Picture ☐

3 In English lessons

doing craft work	playing games	doing exercises

_____ Picture ☐

Extension worksheet 1

Find the people. Number the sentences.

→ = 20

☐	☐	**5** This is the boy who's playing the trumpet and who isn't wearing glasses.	☐ This is the teacher who is standing up.
☐ This is the boy who is playing the trumpet and wearing glasses.	*(music instruments illustration)*		**7** This is the teacher who
☐ This is the girl who is playing the guitar.	☐ This is the girl who is playing the drums and wearing a skirt.	☐	☐ This is the boy who is playing the drums and wearing black trousers.

↓ = 20

= 20

= 20

= 2

Each side → and ↓ = 20. Think and write sentences.

Unit 1

Extension worksheet 2

Read the clues. Write the sentences from the story.

1. The man who is jumping says this.
2. The woman who is eating asks this question.
3. The boy who has his hand up asks this question.
4. Key asks this question when they are leaving the school.
5. Key says this when he is pointing at the ball.
6. Lock says this when we can see three children who are sitting down.

Song worksheet

 Match the words that rhyme. Complete the song.

| need | draw | slow | add | ~~teach~~ |
| go | week | read | floor | sad |

 ▶5 **Listen and check. Sing.**

The classroom's where you learn,

The classroom's where we

_____teach_____ ,

Lots of exciting things,

To do in our school _____ ...

1 I teach Sport,

It's quick, not _____ ,

Run, jump and skip,

Go, go, _____ !

2 I teach English,

All I _____ ,

Are lots of words,

And books to

_____ .

3 I teach Maths,

It's easy to _____ ,

But if it's wrong,

Don't be _____ .

4 I teach Art,

We can paint and _____ ,

Careful with the paint,

Don't drop it on the _____ !

5 The classroom's where you learn,

The classroom's where we

_____ ,

Lots of exciting things,

To do in our school _____ ...

Topic worksheet

 Read about measuring. Do the activities.

In the United Kingdom, people use the metric system to measure, but a lot of people in the United Kingdom and in the United States still use the imperial system from before. Some people still say their height in feet and inches. One foot is about 30 centimetres and there are 12 inches in a foot. One inch is about two and a half centimetres or 25 millimetres.

How many centimetres are there in a metre? ....

How many millimetres are there in a centimetre? ....

How tall are you and your friends and family in feet and inches?

Name	Centimetres	Feet and inches

Television and computer sizes are in inches – and not just in the United Kingdom! Look at these televisions and computers. We write inches like this: 22".

How big are these televisions and computers in centimetres?

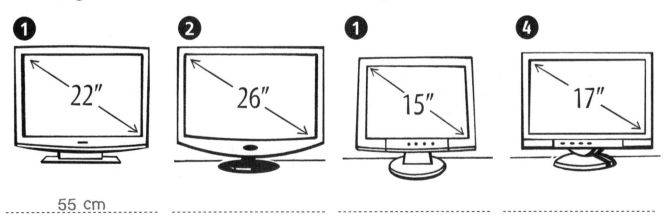

❶ 22"   ❷ 26"   ❶ 15"   ❹ 17"

55 cm ....

Reinforcement worksheet 1

- Pupils look at what each child wants from a summer camp. They read the information to decide which camp is best suited to each child, then write the reasons for their choice. They also give their own preference and explain why.

Key: Daisy: Seaside Camp, Sally: Adventure Camp, Federico: Study Camp.

- *Optional follow-up activity:* Pupils write the publicity for the camp they would like to go to. They can suggest a suitable age range for their chosen camp or give different age limits for the various activities on offer.

Reinforcement worksheet 2

- Pupils colour in the adverbs in the wordsearch. They then copy the remaining letters exactly in the same order as they are in the wordsearch to find four tongue twisters containing adverbs. Help with meaning and make links with the children's literacy studies by talking about alliteration (words beginning with the same sound) and onomatopoeia (words that sound like their meaning). Encourage them to say the tongue twisters faster and faster.

Key: 1 Freshly fried fresh fish, 2 Please pay promptly, 3 Crisp crusts crackle crunchily, 4 Nine nice night nurses nursing nicely nightly.

- *Optional follow-up activity:* In groups, pupils take it in turns to say one (or more) of the tongue twisters. For each tongue twister, the winner is the pupil who says it most quickly without making a mistake.

Extension worksheet 1

- Pupils read the texts and then answer the questions to complete the crossword.

Key: 1 Daisy, 2 Vicky, 3 blue, 4 yellow, 5 library, 6 quickly, 7 slowly.

- *Optional follow-up activity:* Pupils personalise this activity by using the answers to Activity 6 on page 20 of the Activity Book. In groups, the children take it in turns to read their answers whilst the rest make notes. They then design a crossword based on their answers.

Extension worksheet 2

- This can be done as a listening exercise (Track 6) or a reading exercise. If you use the audio recording, pause after each frame while the pupils write. Pupils find the words in the story and replace them with their opposites to correct the story text.

Key: See Pupil's Book, page 23.

- *Optional follow-up activity:* In groups of four, pupils agree on a way to describe each frame, for example, *The picture where Lock is …* Each pupil cuts out the six frames. The dealer shuffles them and deals three to each pupil. The rest are put in a pile in the middle. Pupils look at their own cards but do not show them to the group. Pupil A asks another pupil for a card using the description on which they have agreed. If the pupil has it, he/she must hand it over. Once a player has two frames the same, he/she puts them aside. If he/she does not have it, Pupil A has to pick up one of the cards from the pile. Play continues round the circle. The winner is the player with the most pairs at the end of the game.

Song worksheet

- Pupils solve the anagrams and write in the correct adverbs. They listen to the song (Track 7) to check their answers. They then create more anagrams of words from the song for a friend to solve.

Key: See Pupil's Book, page 21.

- *Optional follow-up activity:* One pupil stands at the front of the class. Show him/her the list of adverbs and ask him/her to choose one. Other pupils name an activity and the child must do the activity in line with the adverb they have chosen. Pupils win points for guessing the adverbs.

Topic worksheet

- Pupils read about the Olympics. They match the pictures with the information about the heptathlon events.

Key: 2 F, 4   3 D, 5   4 E, 6   5 A, 2   6 G, 1   7 B, 7.

- *Optional follow-up activity:* Pupils research the events in the decathlon and prepare a similar table and definitions.

Key: First day: 100 m race, long jump, shot put, high jump, 400 m race. Second day: 110 m hurdles, discus, pole vault, javelin, 1500 m race.

Reinforcement worksheet 1

 Look at the table. Read about the camps. Which camp does each child want to go to?

Daisy: .... Camp   Sally: .... Camp

Federico: .... Camp

Daisy	Sally	Federico
sail ✓	dance ✓	draw ✓
swim ✓	swim ✗	run ✗
climb ✗	play tennis ✗	climb ✗
study ✗	climb ✓	study ✓
fish ✓	skate ✓	play baseball ✓

Adventure Camp

Do you want to do something different this summer? Then this camp is for you. Every morning there are dance and skating lessons and in the afternoons we go for walks in the countryside where you can climb mountains.

Seaside Camp

This camp is great for those who like water sports. You can swim in our fantastic swimming pool and in the sea. There is a river for fishing and a lake for sailing.

Study Camp

Do you want to study English this summer? Come to Study Camp and meet other people your age who want to study English. For even more practice, we teach you how to play a favourite American game: baseball. Drawing classes each day from ten o'clock to eleven o'clock.

 Write about the children.

Daisy wants to sail ... but she doesn't want to ...

....

....

 Which camp do you want to go to? Why?

....

Reinforcement worksheet 2

 Find and colour the adverbs.

| carefully | badly | quietly | well | loudly | slowly | quickly |

f	c	r	e	q	s	h	l	y	f	r	i
e	d	a	f	u	r	e	s	h	f	i	s
h	p	l	r	i	e	a	s	e	p	a	q
y	p	r	o	e	m	p	t	l	y	c	u
s	r	i	s	t	f	p	c	r	u	s	i
l	t	s	c	l	r	u	a	c	k	l	c
o	e	c	r	y	u	n	l	c	h	i	k
w	l	y	n	i	b	a	d	l	y	n	l
l	e	e	n	i	c	e	n	i	y	g	y
y	h	l	t	n	u	r	s	e	s	n	u
r	s	i	l	o	u	d	l	y	n	g	n
i	c	e	l	y	n	i	g	h	t	l	y

 Find the extra letters across (→) the wordsearch.
Write them on the lines to find four tongue twisters.

1 F r e s h l y _ _ _ _ _ _ _ _ _ _ _ _ _ _

2 _ _ _ _ _ _ _ _ _ _ _ _ _ _ _ _

3 _ _ _ _ _ _ _ _ _ _ _ _ _ _ _ _ _ _ _ _ _ _ _ _

4 _ _ _ _ _ _ _ _ _ _ _ _ _ _ _ _ _ _ _ _ _ _ _ _ _ _ _ _ _

_ _ _ _ _ _ _

Say the tongue twisters quickly!

Kid's Box Teacher's Resource Book 4   © Cambridge University Press 2015

Unit 2 Extension worksheet 1

 Read the texts.

In sport, Jack and John are running. Jack runs 100 m in 15 seconds and John runs 50 m in 11 seconds.

Daisy and Sally want to buy a book. It costs £15. They both have £20. First they go to the clothes shop. Daisy buys a cap for £4 and Sally buys a scarf for £8.

Vicky and Mary want to learn to sing. They go to a class. Vicky sings loudly and Mary sings quietly.

The blue team are playing baseball against the yellow team. Paul is in the yellow team. Today his team is playing badly. Jim is playing well. His team is winning.

 Now read the clues and complete the crossword.

Across →

1 This is the girl who can buy the book.

2 This is the girl who you can hear from outside.

3 This is Jim's team.

4 This team isn't winning.

Down ↓

5 Sally must go to the ... for the book because she can't buy it.

6 Jack is the boy who runs ... .

7 John is the boy who runs ... .

© Cambridge University Press 2015   Kid's Box Teacher's Resource Book 4

Extension worksheet 2

 Find the words in the story. Cross them out and write the opposite.

~~dirty~~ quietly ugly small She's Don't help me easy

clean

Kid's Box Teacher's Resource Book 4 © Cambridge University Press 2015 **PHOTOCOPIABLE**

Unit 2 Song worksheet

 Correct the strange words.

Activity centre,
Lots of fun.
A place to skate,
Sail and run.
Activity centre …

Activity centre,
Lots of fun.
A place to skate,
Sail and run.
Activity centre …

3 We're sailing piphaly,

Our boat's short.

We're going lowsly,

What a great sport.

1 I'm skating well,

Round and round.

qu
I'm moving ~~kucialy,~~

Over the ground.

2 I'm climbing aisely,

Up the wall.

I'm going flareculy,

So I don't fall.

Activity centre,
Lots of fun.
A place to skate,
Sail and run.
Activity centre …

Activity centre,
Lots of fun.
A place to skate,
Sail and run.
Activity centre …

7 **Listen and check. Sing. Write more strange words for your friend to find.**

© Cambridge University Press 2015   Kid's Box Teacher's Resource Book 4   **27**

Topic worksheet

 Read about events at the Olympics.

There was only one race in the first Olympic Games in Greece in 776 BC. It was 192 metres long. The first modern Olympic Games with different countries were in 1896. They were Pierre de Coubertain's idea. He was a French man. Now, there are many different events. In the decathlon, men run, jump and throw things in ten events. In the heptathlon, for women, there are seven events.

 Match the pictures and the information with the heptathlon events.

Heptathlon: First day	Heptathlon: Second day
1 100 m hurdles: C, 3	**5** Long jump:
2 High jump:	**6** Javelin:
3 Shot put:	**7** 800 m race:
4 200 m race:	

❶ The thing that you throw is between 220 and 230 cm long.

❷ You must jump as far as possible.

❸ You must run and jump over ten things.

❹ You must jump as high as possible.

❺ You must throw a metal ball as far as possible.

❻ You must run half way round the track.

❼ You must run round the track two times.

Kid's Box Teacher's Resource Book 4   © Cambridge University Press 2015

3 Teacher's notes

Reinforcement worksheet 1

- Pupils follow the drawing instructions, answer the question and colour the squares to show the verb pairs.

Key: A star.

- *Optional follow-up activity:* Pupils think of a different shape/route and write the instructions for a friend.

Reinforcement worksheet 2

- Pupils use the visual clues to complete the postcards.

Key: 2 it was sunny, 3 We went in the sea, 4 we were hungry, 5 we drank a lot, 6 we were thirsty, 7 we went to bed, 8 we were tired, 9 I went to the doctor, 10 I had a cold, 11 gave me some medicine, 12 a temperature and an earache, 13 drank a lot, 14 I was hot and thirsty.

- *Optional follow-up activity:* Pupils write a postcard to include at least two *because* clauses. They 'send' them to a friend who can then read the text aloud.

Extension worksheet 1

- It is easier to give each group a dice, but if you haven't got enough, ask them to cut out the spinner, mount it on card and push a pencil through the centre. Pupils also need two counters each, which they can cut out from the worksheet too.

- They throw the dice or spin the spinner twice and count that number of spaces. With the first throw/spin, they put one counter on an adjective and with the second, they put their other counter on a verb. They combine the two to make a sentence, which will make more or less sense depending on the combination! They continue to move up and down the adjective and verb lines with their two counters to form new sentences. If you would like the class to do the optional follow-up activity, ask the pupils to write the sentences that they form.

- *Optional follow-up activity:* In groups, Pupil A begins to read a sentence from the game on the worksheet but stops after *because*. The rest check whether they made a sentence with that verb and those who did take it in turns to read the second half of the sentence. Pupil A decides which sentence he/she prefers. That pupil begins the next sentence.

Extension worksheet 2

- This can be done as a listening exercise (Track 8) or a reading exercise. If you use the audio recording, pause after each frame while the pupils write. Pupils insert the missing vowels. Ask them to count the number of times they have written each letter.

Key: See Pupil's Book, page 33.
A 30, E 51, I 37, O 48, U 6.

- *Optional follow-up activity:* Give pupils two minutes to write as many words as possible beginning with *a* and *o*. The winner is the pupil with the most words.

Song worksheet

- Pupils look at the definitions and write the words. They then use these words to complete the song. They listen to the song (Track 9) to check their answers.

Key: See Pupil's Book, page 31.

- *Optional follow-up activity:* Pupils draw a 12 X 12 grid in their notebooks and design a wordsearch to contain the ten words from the exercise. They swap them with a friend.

Topic worksheet

- Pre-teach words you think the pupils may find difficult and encourage them to look at the pictures to help their understanding. Pupils read the text.

- Pupils design a poster to advertise a concert by the Recycled Orchestra. Remind them to write where and when it will be. They should include some drawings of recyled instruments

- In small groups, pupils decide on their favourite poster and then do the same at a whole-class level.

- *Optional follow-up activity:* Show the film of the Recycled Orchestra found on the internet (also called the landfillharmonic).

 Follow the instructions. What shape can you see?

Draw a line from the past of 'be' to the past of 'see'.

Draw a line from the past of 'go' to the past of 'give'.

Draw a line from the past of 'drink' to the past of 'have'.

Draw a line from the past of 'take' to the past of 'eat'.

Draw a line from the past of 'drink' to the past of 'see'.

Draw a line from the past of 'go' to the past of 'have'.

Draw a line from the past of 'take' to the past of 'be'.

Draw a line from the past of 'give' to the past of 'eat'.

see	do	was / were	did	have	eat
drank	saw	give	drink	took	ate
go	had	take / went		gave	be

 Colour the pairs of verbs (past/present) the same colour.

Kid's Box Teacher's Resource Book 4 © Cambridge University Press 2015

Reinforcement worsheet 2

 Look at the pictures. Complete the postcards.

> We went in the sea   it was sunny   we drank a lot   we went to bed
> we were hungry   we were tired   we were thirsty   ~~I went to the beach~~

Dear Grandma,

On Thursday, (1) <u>I went to the beach</u> with my friends

because (2) _____ . (3) _____

because it was hot and then we ate a lot because

(4) _____ and (5) _____ because

(6) _____ . At night, (7) _____

early because (8) _____ .

Love,

Mary

Mrs

50 S

Bris

BS2

> I had a cold   gave me some medicine   I went to the doctor
> I was hot and thirsty   a temperature and an earache   drank a lot

Dear Grandad,

Yesterday (9) _____ because

(10) _____ . The doctor (11) _____

_____ because I had (12) _____

_____ . I (13) _____ of water because

(14) _____ . Now I'm better.

Love,

Paul

Mr

1 R

Lon

© Cambridge University Press 2015   Kid's Box Teacher's Resource Book 4

Unit 3 Extension worksheet 1

 Play the game.

Move up and down the lines. Write the words where you land.

Make sentences. They can be funny.

I **ate** a sandwich **because** I was **afraid**!

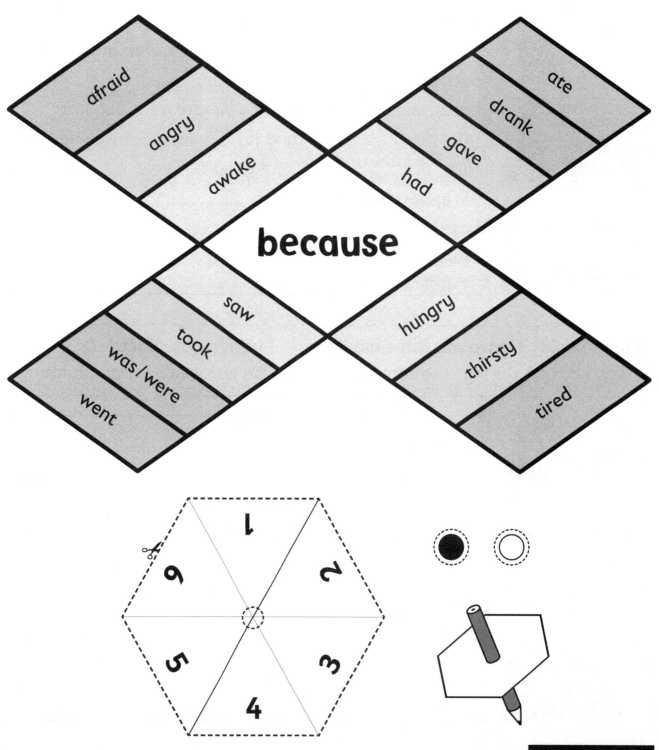

afraid
angry
awake

ate
drank
gave
had

because

saw
took
was/were
went

hungry
thirsty
tired

1 2 3 4 5 6

Kid's Box Teacher's Resource Book 4   © Cambridge University Press 2015   **PHOTOCOPIABLE**

Extension worksheet 2

⭐ **Complete the story.**

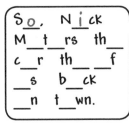

S_o_, N_i_ck
M_t_rs th_
c_r th_ _ _f
_s b_ck
_n t_wn.

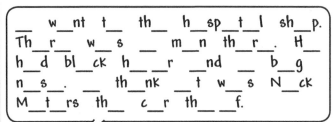

_ _ w_nt t_ th_ h_sp_t_l sh_p.
Th_r_ w_s _ m_n th_r_. H_
h_d bl_ck h_ _r _nd _ b_g
n_s_. _ th_nk _t w_s N_ck
M_t_rs th_ c_r th_ _ _f.

_ _ _ _ _ _ps! S_rry _'m l_t_.
_ w_nt t_ th_ h_sp_t_l t_
s_ _ my _ _nt _mm_. Sh_'s
g_t _ b_d c_ _ _gh.

_n th_
h_sp_t_l?
L_t's g_
th_r_ n_w.

_ _r_ _lly w_nt t_ c_tch
N_ck M_t_rs th_s t_m_, K_y.

C_m_ _n! W_ n_ _d t_ g_
_ns_d_ q_ _ _ckly b_f_r_ h_
r_ns _w_y.

N_ _ pr_bl_m,
L_ck!

Th_r_ h_ _s!
Th_t's h_m, L_ck!

N_ck M_t_rs _sn't _ns_d_
th_ h_sp_t_l, K_y. H_'s
_ _t s_d_ _n th_ str_ _ _t...
_nd ...

N_ K_y,
h_'s n_t
N_ck M_t_rs.
H_'s _
d_ct_r.

H_'s t_k_ng
_ _ _r
m_t_rb_k_!

Unit 3

Song worksheet

⭐ **Think and write. Complete the song.**

This is the opposite of 'slow'. …quick…

One and two make ……………………… .

This is the past of 'do'. ……………………

Apples, oranges and bananas are all ……………………… .

This person helps you. He or she works with a doctor. ……………………

People eat this more in summer than in winter. ……………………

This is the infinitive of 'drank'. ……………………

You get this when you eat too much. ……………………

Today is Thursday. …………………… was Wednesday.

This is the infinitive of 'ate'. ……………………

Mummy, Mummy, call the
(1) …………………… !
I had a (2) …………………… but now
it's worse.
What's the matter?
I don't know, but please be (3) …quick… ,
Don't be slow.
Did you have a party (4) …………………… ?
Yes. There was lots to eat and games
to play.
(5) …………………… you eat burgers?
Yes, I did.
Did you (6) …………………… sausages?
Yes, I did.
Did you (7) …………………… lemonade?
Yes, I did.

Did you have (8) ……………………
and chocolate too?
I think I know what's the matter
with you!
Take this medicine (9) ……………………
times a day,
When you are better, go out
and play!
No more chocolate cake for you
my daughter.
Vegetables, (10) ……………………
and a drink of water!

⭐ ▶9 **Listen and check.
Sing.**

Topic worksheet

 Read about the 'Recycled Orchestra'.

The 'Recycled Orchestra' is the name of a very special children's orchestra. All the instruments are made out of rubbish! The orchestra comes from the town of Cateura in Paraguay and all the musicians live nearby. The director of the orchestra is Favio Chávez. Favio also works at the rubbish dump. He teaches music to children in the town.

A lot of children came to Favio's lessons to learn music. There were a lot of children but there weren't a lot of instruments! Favio had an idea to make instruments from rubbish! Now, the children don't have to buy new instruments to play in the orchestra. They make violins, cellos and other instruments from old paint and oil cans, wood and other rubbish. All the instruments are recycled!

Now there are 35 children in the orchestra. They work very hard. They travel to different countries around the world to play in concerts. People love watching them!

 Make a poster for a 'Recycled Orchestra' concert. Draw pictures of some instruments. Remember to put where the concert is and when it is.

Teacher's notes

Reinforcement worksheet 1

- Pupils use the co-ordinate key to work out the verbs. They transfer them to the correct column of the table and complete the missing forms.

Key: b play – 2 played, 3 help – c helped, 4 carry – d carried, e stop – 5 stopped, f dance – 6 danced, 7 hop – g hopped.

- *Optional follow-up activity:* Pupils make a new co-ordinate key with all the letters of the alphabet to write a secret message for a friend.

Reinforcement worksheet 2

- Pupils decide which verb goes with each picture. They use the information to complete the text. They write questions and answers about Jane's week.

Key: c second, d danced, e third, f hopped, g fourth, h carried, i fifth, j helped, k sixth, l stopped, m seventh, n laughed.

- *Optional follow-up activity:* In groups of seven, each pupil has a sheet of paper and writes at the top of the page, *On the first day I ...* and continues the sentence. They then fold over the paper so that the sentence is hidden and pass the paper to the pupil on their left. Each pupil then writes, beneath the fold, *On the second day, I ...* This continues until each pupil has written one sentence on each sheet of paper. Pupils take it in turns to unfold the paper and read about a complete week. They decide which week is the most exciting, amusing, etc.

Extension worksheet 1

- Pupils complete the table, dividing the past verb forms into three groups according to their final sound: /t/, /d/ or /ɪd/. They then follow the instructions to write sentences using certain verbs from the table.

Key: /t/– danced, stopped, helped, /d/– climbed, played, lived, loved, /ɪd/– shouted, started, painted, invited. Pupils' own sentences with: *(climbed), painted, helped, played.*

- *Optional follow-up activity:* In groups, pupils read out their sentences and decide which one they like best. They then illustrate the chosen sentence as a pronunciation reminder. Display the pictures in three groups according to the final sound.

Extension worksheet 2

- Pupils listen to the story (Track 10) and follow on the worksheet. They then follow the instructions to write the sentences from the story. They can write in their notebooks or on the back of the worksheet, as you prefer.

Key: See Pupil's Book, page 41.

- *Optional follow-up activity:* In groups of four, each pupil cuts out the six frames. The dealer shuffles them and deals them all out. Pupil A puts one of the frames face up on the table and the others race to put down the next frame. The first to do so keeps the cards and play passes to Pupil B, and so on. The game continues until one pupil has won all the cards. Tell the pupils that, in this game, frame 1 follows on from frame 6.

Song worksheet

- Pupils first negotiate with the group whether they can complete the gaps in any order or whether everyone must work through from first to twelfth. They then throw one dice until they have thrown 1–6 and then two together to enable them to throw 7–12. They complete the song with ordinal numbers as they throw the corresponding number on the dice. They keep a record of how many throws they need to complete it.

- When everyone is ready, they listen to the song (Track 11) to check their answers.

Key: second, third, fourth, fifth, sixth, seventh, eighth, ninth, tenth, eleventh, twelfth.

- *Optional follow-up activity:* In groups, pupils adapt the lyrics to another activity, e.g. playing football instead of dancing. They take it in turns to sing and mime the actions.

Topic worksheet

- Pupils make a mini book in class by folding along the solid lines (first fold 1, after which they cut along the dotted lines, then fold 2 and the remaining two lines). When all the folds have been made, they open the sheet up again and fold along fold 2 again. They then join point a to point b, point c to point d and, finally, point e to point f. Once they have made the book, they write their own mini story and decide on a title for it.

- *Optional follow-up activity:* Pupils take it in turns to read their stories aloud.

Reinforcement worksheet 1

 Think and write.

	A	B	C	D	E	F
6	r	l	e	s	r	a
5	t	y	o	d	u	h
4	e	g	d	h	a	p
3	p	l	p	p	e	n
2	c	d	e	l	h	a
1	c	o	y	d	a	p

 Use the code to find the verbs. Complete the table.

1 B6-F6-E5-B4-D4

2 C3-B3-F2-C1-A4-D1

3 E2-C6-D2-F4

4 A1-E4-A6-E6-B5

5 D6-A5-B1-C3-F1-E3-B2

6 C4-E1-F3-A2-C2-D5

7 F5-C5-A3

Infinitive	Past
1 laugh	a laughed
b	2
3	c
4	d
e	5
f	6
7	g

© Cambridge University Press 2015   Kid's Box Teacher's Resource Book 4

Reinforcement worksheet 2

 Match the pictures with the verbs.

| helped | laughed | played | danced | ~~stopped~~ | hopped | carried |

1 **2** **3** **4** **5** **6** **7**

..stopped.. ....

 Use the information to complete the text.

1st day	2nd day	3rd day	4th day	5th day	6th day	7th day
Picture 7	Picture 3	Picture 4	Picture 2	Picture 5	Picture 1	Picture 6

Jane was on holiday. She had an exciting week.

On the (a) __first__ day, she (b) __played__ tennis with her friends.

On the (c) _____ day, she (d) _____ . On the

(e) _____ day, she (f) _____ in the park. On the

(g) _____ day, she (h) _____ her baby cousin. On the

(i) _____ day, she (j) _____ a woman to cross the

road. On the (k) _____ day, she (l) _____ her little

brother from crossing the road. Her mum was happy. She gave Jane a ticket

for the circus so on the (m) _____ day, she went to the circus

where she (n) _____ a lot.

 Ask Jane questions about her week. Write her answers.

Did you carry your cousin on the first day? No, I didn't. ....

Unit 4

Extension worksheet 1

 Say the verbs. Think about the final sound. Complete the table.

laughed climbed played shouted danced stopped
lived started helped painted loved invited

Pat /t/	Tod /d/	David /ɪd/
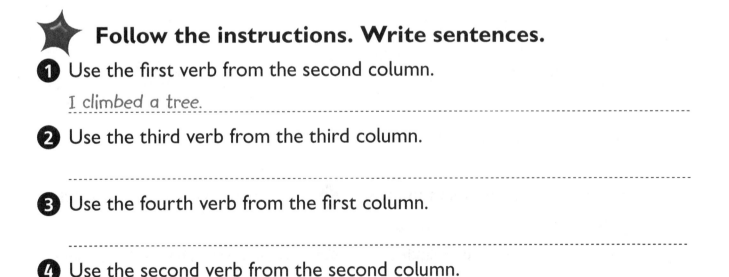		
laughed		

Follow the instructions. Write sentences.

1 Use the first verb from the second column.

I climbed a tree.

2 Use the third verb from the third column.

3 Use the fourth verb from the first column.

4 Use the second verb from the second column.

© Cambridge University Press 2015   Kid's Box Teacher's Resource Book 4

Extension worksheet 2

 Read the clues. Write the sentences from the story.

1. Lock asks Key this when they are going to their chairs.
2. The man with the beard and the hat says this when he is standing up.
3. Key says this when he is drinking the lemonade.
4. Peter's dad says this when he is on the floor.
5. Peter asks this when he is walking through the door.
6. Key asks this when Peter is giving him the tickets.

Song worksheet

 Throw the dice and write the correct ordinal numbers.

Dancing is good, dancing is fine,

Dancing is great!

Come on, children! Dance in line!

.... First ...., ...,

.... and ....

Dance, dance across the floor.

..........................., ...,

..........................., ...

Jump, kick, don't come in late.

..........................., ...,

..........................., ...

Dancing is good for your health.

Dancing's good, dancing's fine,

Come on, children! Dance in line!

Number five's first,

And number ten's last.

He can't hop and skip,

He can't get past.

Dancing is good, dancing is fine,

Dancing is great!

Come on, children! Dance in line.

 How many times did you throw the dice?

 🔟 **Listen and check. Sing.**

Unit 4 Topic worksheet

 Make and write a book.

fold 2

One day, he / she

_ _ _ _ _ _ _ _ _ _ _ _ _ _ _

Then, he / she

_ _ _ _ _ _ _ _ _ _ _ _ _ _ _

Then, he / she

_ _ _ _ _ _ _ _ _ _ _ _ _ _ _

In the end, he / she

_ _ _ _ _ _ _ _ _ _ _ _ _ _ _

by

_ _ _ _ _ _ _ _ _ _ _ _ _ _ _

e •

f •

and he / she

_ _ _ _ _ _ _ _ _ _ _ _ _ _ _

was _ _ _ _ _ _ _ _ _ _ _ _

because _ _ _ _ _ _ _ _ _ _

He / She was

_ _ _ _ _ _ _ _ _ _ _ _ _ _ _

because _ _ _ _ _ _ _ _ _ _

He / She lived in

_ _ _ _ _ _ _ _ _ _ _ _ _ _ _

Once upon a time
there was a

_ _ _ _ _ _ _ _ _ _ _ _ _ _ _

b •

a •

d •

c •

fold 1

5 Teacher's notes

Reinforcement worksheet 1

- Pupils count forwards and backwards along the alphabet to find the past verb forms. They transfer them to the table and write in the infinitives.

Key: 2 go – went, 3 lose – lost, 4 have – had, 5 find – found, 6 take – took, 7 can – could, 8 get – got, 9 make – made.

- *Optional follow-up activity:* Pupils write a mystery message in the same way for a friend. Tell them to start the code for each new word on a separate line.

Reinforcement worksheet 2

- It is best to photocopy this worksheet onto card. Pupils make two spinners by cutting out the shapes and pushing a pencil through the centre of each one. They spin Spinner 1 to write the first part of the sentence and Spinner 2 for the clause after *so*. They then tick the sentences if the combination makes sense and cross them if they don't.

- *Optional follow-up activity:* Pupils work in pairs, A and B. They take it in turns to spin Spinner 1 then they both spin Spinner 2. The pupil whose sentence makes most sense gets a point. The winner is the player with the most points.

Extension worksheet 1

- Pupils decide which two items from the wordpool go with each picture. They then use the pictures and the adjectives below each one to write comparative sentences giving their own ideas.

Key: 2 shopping, visiting museums; 3 the Eiffel Tower, the Pyramids; 4 the man, the boy; 5 the girl, the woman; 6 Antarctica, the beach; 7 English, Chinese.

- *Optional follow-up activity:* Pupils work in groups and play *Chinese whispers*. They stand in a line or sit in a circle. One child first whispers to you (or shows you) one of his/her comparative sentences. He/She then whispers it to the child next to him/her, who then whispers it to the next person, etc. The last child in the group says the sentence aloud. The sentence is compared with the original and pupils give each other a high five if they've got it right. They can then reorganise the group to play again. If you wish, two teams can play against each other.

Extension worksheet 2

- This can be done as a listening exercise (Track 12) or a reading exercise. If you use the audio recording, pause after each frame while the pupils write. Pupils find the words in the story and replace them with their opposites to correct the story text.

Key: See Pupil's Book, page 51.

- *Optional follow-up activity:* In groups of four, pupils agree on a way to describe each frame, for example, *The picture where Lock is …* Each pupil cuts out the six frames. The dealer shuffles them and deals three to each pupil. The rest are put in a pile in the middle. Pupils look at their own cards but do not show them to the group. Pupil A asks another pupil for a card using the description on which they have agreed. If the pupil has it, he/she must hand it over. Once a player has two frames the same, he/she puts them aside. If he/she does not have it, Pupil A has to pick up one of the cards from the pile. Play continues round the circle. The winner is the player with the most pairs at the end of the game.

Song worksheet

- Pupils first match the rhyming words. They then complete the rap with the rhyming words, thinking carefully about sense. They listen to the rap (Track 13) to check their answers.

Key: See Pupil's Book, page 50.

- *Optional follow-up activity:* In small groups, the pupils design posters for the classroom or school display area. They can use any suitable language but encourage them to use phrases from the rap, both to include everybody, such as *The world is ours / This is our world*, and to encourage responsible care for the environment, such as *Let's keep it clean.*

Topic worksheet

- In pairs, pupils write a mixture of eleven statements saying things you do that are good for the Earth and things you do that are bad for the Earth. Then refer them to the boxes of game instructions at the bottom of the worksheet and check comprehension. Following the example, they decide where to put each sentence and instruction. They decorate and colour their board game and design four counters. They also need dice. They play each other's games in small groups.

- *Optional follow-up activity:* Pupils write sentences for a different game with good and bad practice in the classroom, e.g. speaking English, bringing their books, putting their hands up, etc.

Reinforcement worksheet 1

⭐ **Find the words.**

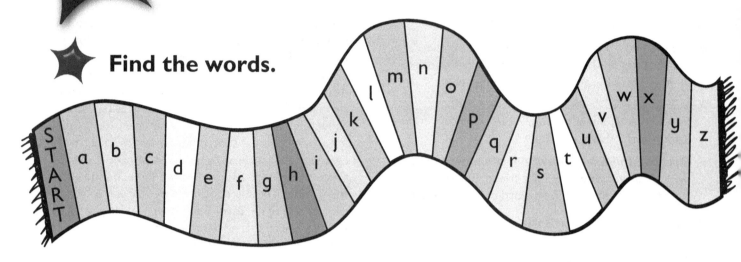

1 Count 3 from the start. Go back 2.
Go forward 20. Go back 14.
Go forward 1. Go forward 12.
<u>c a u g h t</u>

2 Count 23 from the start. Go back 18.
Go forward 9. Go forward 6.
_ _ _ _

3 Count 12 from the start.
Go forward 3. Go forward 4.
Go forward 1. _ _ _ _

4 Count 8 from the start. Go back 7.
Go forward 3. _ _ _

5 Count 6 from the start.
Go forward 9. Go forward 6.
Go back 7. Go back 10. _ _ _ _ _ _

6 Count 20 from the start. Go back 5.
Don't move. Go back 4. _ _ _ _ _

7 Count 3 from the start.
Go forward 12. Go forward 6.
Go back 9. Go back 8. _ _ _ _ _

8 Count 7 from the start.
Go forward 8. Go forward 5.
_ _ _

9 Count 13 from the start.
Go back 12. Go forward 3.
Go forward 1. _ _ _ _

 Complete the table.

Infinitive	Past
❶ catch	caught
❷	
❸	
❹	
❺	
❻	
❼	
❽	
❾	

 Kid's Box Teacher's Resource Book 4 **PHOTOCOPIABLE**

★ **Play the game. Write sentences. Put a tick (✓) or a cross (✗).**

1 They were hungry so he went out to play. .... ✗

2 They were hungry so they ate lots of food. .... ✓

3 .... ☐

4 .... ☐

5 .... ☐

6 .... ☐

7 .... ☐

8 .... ☐

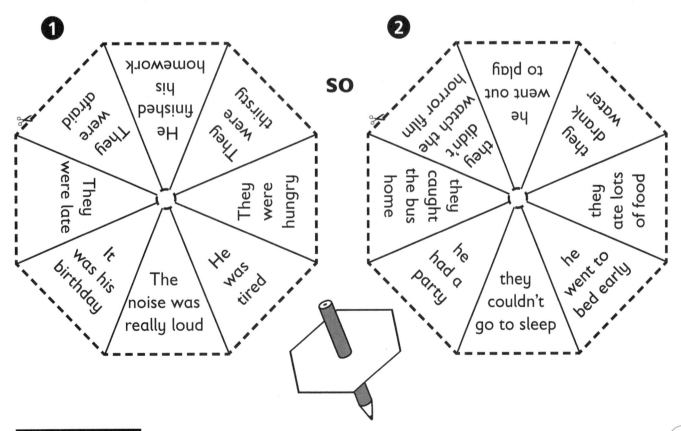

1

They were afraid
He finished his homework
They were thirsty
They were late
It was his birthday
The noise was really loud
He was tired
They were hungry

SO

2

they didn't watch the horror film
he went out to play
they drank water
they caught the bus home
they ate lots of food
he had a party
they couldn't go to sleep
he went to bed early

Unit 5

Extension worksheet 1

 Match the words with the pictures.

| Antarctica the boy English ~~football~~ shopping visiting museums the Pyramids the girl the man the woman Chinese the Eiffel Tower ~~tennis~~ the beach |

1 (boring)

football

tennis

2 (exciting)

3 (famous)

4 (careful)

5 (tired)

6 (beautiful)

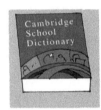 

7 (difficult)

What do you think? Write sentences.

1 --

2 --

3 --

4 --

5 --

6 --

7 --

Kid's Box Teacher's Resource Book 4   © Cambridge University Press 2015

Extension worksheet 2

⭐ Find the words in the story. Cross them out and write the opposite.

~~morning~~   Goodbye   Thank you   in front of   city
we don't have to   boring   he's here now   Poor

Look, Key! I've got information about Nick Motors. He's on an adventure holiday in the city.

Good! These holidays are more boring than holidays at the beach.

E-mail

Explore Adventure Holidays

Explore Adventure Holidays

Look here. It says you can explore forests, rivers and beaches. Can we go, Lock? Thank you!

days

OK, Key. But we don't have to catch Nick Motors!

He came here yesterday. He caught a bus in the ~~morning~~ and had dinner in the Lakeside Restaurant.

LAKESIDE RESTAURANT

Explore Adventure Holiday Camp

We can catch him easily, Lock. No problem.

afternoon

Excuse me. Do you know this man?

Oh yes! I gave him his breakfast this morning.

Lakeside Menu

Hmmm, but he's here now.

Goodbye! What are you doing here, Mr Key?

LAKESIDE RESTAURANT

Hello, Miss Poor. We're at work. We're trying to catch a thief.

I've got a message on my phone!

I don't understand. It says, 'Look in front of you!'

He's got our bike! I need a holiday.

Song worksheet

 Match the words that rhyme. Complete the rap.

strong	trees	green	~~mistakes~~
lakes	clean	song	seas

The world isn't mine,
The world isn't yours.
The world isn't his,
The world isn't hers.
It's ours,
It's ours!

Our world is tired, we're making ....mistakes....... ,
We need our seas, we need our ....
Our world is weak, we can make it .... ,
It needs our help. Listen to our ....

We must look after its forests and .... ,
We must look after its rivers and ....
We can make it better, we can make it .... ,
This is our world, let's keep it ....
The world isn't mine, …

  Listen and check. Rap.

Kid's Box Teacher's Resource Book 4   © Cambridge University Press 2015   **PHOTOCOPIABLE**

Make and play a game. Invent the instructions.

When do you help the world? When don't you help the world?

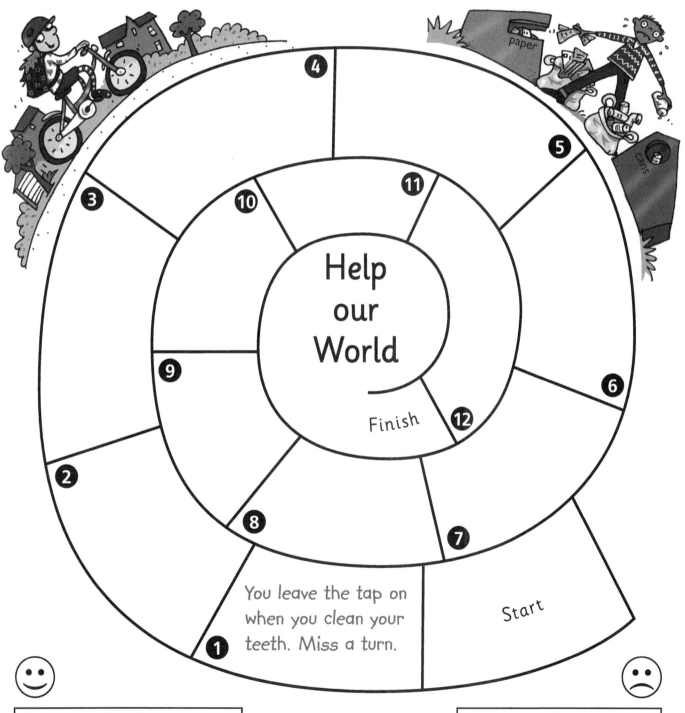

Help our World

Finish

You leave the tap on when you clean your teeth. Miss a turn.

Start

Go forward (1, 2, …) spaces. Throw again.

Go back (1, 2, …) spaces. Miss a turn.

6 Teacher's notes

Reinforcement worksheet 1

- Pupils use the Semaphore (international flag language) code to find the words. They then complete the sentences.

  Key: 2 video, 3 email, 4 button, 5 program, 6 internet. 2 internet, 3 video, DVD, 4 email.

- *Optional follow-up activity:* In groups, each pupil chooses a word from the Pupil's Book and puts it into the international flag language. They tell the rest what page it is on and the first to read it and find it gets a point. The winner is the pupil with the most points.

Reinforcement worksheet 2

- Pupils solve the anagrams and write the infinitives on the lines. They then complete the crossword with past tense verbs. They follow the instructions to work on the sounds in the past tense verbs.

  Key: 2 brought, 3 read, 4 thought, 5 said, 6 put, 7 knew, 8 chose.
  1 brought, thought, 2 read, 3 put.

- *Optional follow-up activity:* Pupils write questions and answers using the verbs from the crossword, e.g. *What did you say? I said, 'Hello!'*

Extension worksheet 1

- Pupils look at the pictures of the three characters and decide which answers they think each would give. Explain that any answers are correct as long as the time makes sense with the clocks shown. They then use the options to write a short text about themselves. They can write in their notebooks or on the back of the worksheet, as you prefer.

- *Optional follow-up activity:* In groups, pupils ask the questions and record their answers on a bar chart. They then compare their bar charts with those of other groups to see how similar they are and how different.

Extension worksheet 2

- This can be done as a listening exercise (Track 14) or a reading exercise. If you use the audio recording, pause after each frame while the pupils write. Pupils insert the missing vowels. Ask them to count the number of times they have written each letter.

  Key: See Pupil's Book, page 59.
  A 40, E 54, I 27, O 61, U 9.

- *Optional follow-up activity:* Give pupils two minutes to write as many words as possible beginning with *i* and *u*. The winner is the pupil with the most words.

Song worksheet

- Pupils match the children's lines with Grandpa's responses. They listen to the song (Track 15) to check their answers.

  Key: See Pupil's Book, page 55.

- *Optional follow-up activity:* In groups, pupils invent a verse about Grandpa's need for a new computer.

Topic worksheet

- Remind your pupils about what they have read about machines and technology. Explain that there are lots of advantages but also some disadvantages.

- Ask them to number the sentences from 1-7 for the advantages and 1-7 for the disadvantages (they should give '1' to the strongest advantage and '1' to the strongest disadvantage).

- Pupils compare their answers with those of their classmates.

- *Optional follow-up activity:* Ask your pupils to transfer the information onto a chart to have a visual representation of their preferences. If you can, compare the answers with those of children in a different class.

 This is 'Semaphore', the international flag language.

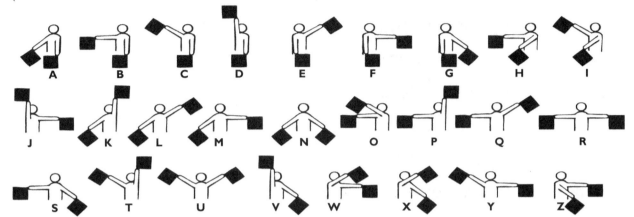

 Use the key to find the words.

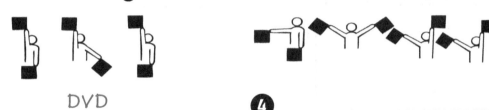

1 _____DVD_____

4 _____

2 _____

5 _____

3 _____

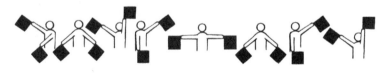

6 _____

 Complete the sentences with five words from above.

1 Which _____button_____ do I need to press?

2 You can find lots of information on the _____ .

3 My parents watched _____s but now I watch _____s.

4 Using _____ is quicker than writing letters.

Reinforcement worksheet 2

⭐ **Find the words. Complete the past tense crossword.**

Number 1 is the past of **uby**.   _____ buy _____

Number 2 is the past of **nrbgi**.   _____

Number 3 is the past of **dear**.   _____

Number 4 is the past of **khint**.   _____

Number 5 is the past of **yas**.   _____

Number 6 is the past of **tup**.   _____

Number 7 is the past of **ownk**.   _____

Number 8 is the past of **oschoe**.   _____

```
                    1
                    b
                    o
    2   3           u           4
                    g
                    h
5                   t       6           7
                                  8
```

⭐ **Look at the past verbs in the crossword.**

❶ Find two verbs that rhyme with 'bought'. _____ , _____

❷ Find a verb that rhymes with 'said'. _____

❸ Which verb sounds the same in the present and the past? _____

Kid's Box Teacher's Resource Book 4   © Cambridge University Press 2015

Unit 6 Extension worksheet 1

 Look at the pictures. What do you think? Read and decide on each child's answers.

Dan	Emma	Ross

Dan		Emma		Ross	
❶ c	❹ ☐	❶ ☐	❹ ☐	❶ ☐	❹ ☐
❷ ☐	❺ ☐	❷ ☐	❺ ☐	❷ ☐	❺ ☐
❸ ☐	❻ ☐	❸ ☐	❻ ☐	❸ ☐	❻ ☐

❶ What time did you get up on Saturday?
   A I got up at eight o'clock.
   B I got up at nine o'clock.
   C I got up at ten o'clock.

❷ What time did you get dressed?
   A I got dressed at nine o'clock.
   B I got dressed at ten o'clock.
   C I got dressed at eleven o'clock.

❸ What did you have for breakfast?
   A I had cakes and biscuits.
   B I didn't have anything.
   C I had fruit.

❹ Did you do any sport?
   A No, I didn't.
   B Yes, I did some.
   C Yes, I did lots of sport.

❺ Did you play on the computer on Saturday?
   A Yes, for more than two hours.
   B Yes, for one to two hours.
   C No, I didn't.

❻ Did you watch DVDs or videos at the weekend?
   A Yes, I watched more than three.
   B Yes, I watched one.
   C No, I didn't.

© Cambridge University Press 2015   Kid's Box Teacher's Resource Book 4

Extension worksheet 2

Complete the story.

I ne e d
y_ _ _ r h_lp.

Wh_ _ t c_n w_
d_ _ f_ _ r y_ _ _,
M_ss R_ch?

_ _ m_n c_m_
_ _nt_ my
b_ _ _t _nd
t_ _ k _ _ ll
th_ m_n_ _y.
Y_ _ _ m_st
c_tch h_ _m!

N_ _ pr_ _bl_ _m, M_ss R_ch!

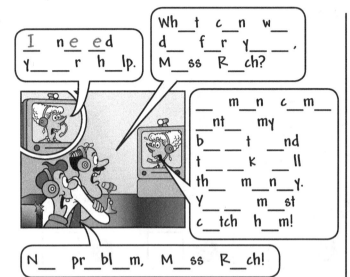

Th_ _ m_n_ _y w_s f_ _r my 'S_v_
Th_ S_ _ _ S_c_ _ty'. H_r_'s
th_ DVD _ f th_ _ _ns_d_ _ _f
th_ b_ _ _t.

L_t's l_ _ _k
_t _ _t.

_ _ _ _ _ _ ps!

_ h_d th_ m_n_ _y _n _
b_g r_ _ _dy t_ p_t _nt_ th_
b_nk. _t w_s _n th_ t_bl_.

H_r_'s th_
m_n_n_w.

_ t's N_ck
M_t_rs!

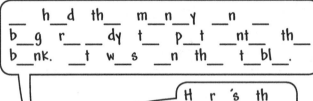

S_ _ N_ck
M_t_rs _s
m_r_ th_n
_ _ c_r
th_ _ _f!

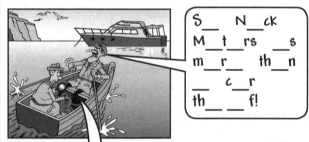

W_ _ll, c_rs _r_ m_r_
d_ff_c_lt t_ _t_k_ th_n
m_n_ _y.

H_ _y! M_t_rs wr_t_ _ _n
_ m_ _ _ l. W_ c_n r_ _ _d _t!

_ _r, L_ck, _ _
th_nk y_ _ _
n_ _ _d t_
l_ _ k_ _ _ t
t_ _s _ _ _!

_h! _ _ _gh!

N_ _ _ _ _ _ _!
H_'s g_t
_ _ r b_ _ _t,
t _ _ _!

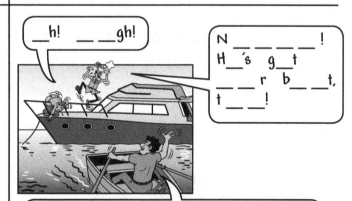

By_ _by_ _ b_ _ys! Th_ w_t_r's
l_v_ly! H_v_ _ _ n_c_ _ sw_m!

Unit 6

Song worksheet

 Match the lines of the song.

1 Grandpa needs a new mobile,

2 With an MP3.

3 It's got music and video clips,
And lots, lots more to see.

a (A what?)

b (No, I don't!)

c (I don't need any more!)

4 Grandpa needs a new mobile,

5 So he can text his friends.

6 He can take lots of photos,
And play games at weekends.

d (I go fishing at weekends!)

e (No, I don't!)

f (I can talk to my friends!)

Grandpa!

Grandpa!

Grandpa!

Grandpa needs a new mobile.

(I've got a DVD player at home!)

(I've got a nice camera!)

(And my old mobile phone works perfectly well!)

(A new mobile phone!)

7 Grandpa needs a new mobile,

8 So he can plan his day.

9 He can listen to lots of songs,
And phone or even play.

g (I haven't got time to play!
I've got a radio! I've got a nice camera! My old mobile phone works perfectly well! Hmph!)

h (I've got a pen and paper!)

i (No, I don't!)

 15 Listen and check. Sing.

6 Topic worksheet

 Read the sentences. Number the advantages and the disadvantages of modern technology from 1–7.

Advantages

☐ You can use the internet to get information.

☐ You can use fast trains and planes to travel a long way quickly.

☐ Machines do work in the house like wash our clothes, wash the plates and clean the floor.

☐ Talking is easier because of mobile phones and the internet.

☐ Robots in factories are a good idea because they don't get bored or ill.

☐ Doctors can save more lives now because they use a lot of machines.

☐ Robots do jobs which humans can't do because they are very difficult or dangerous.

Disadvantages

☐ People lose their jobs because machines are cheaper than humans and work more quickly.

☐ People don't think a lot because they use computers to do Maths and answer questions.

☐ When we make and use machines, we make the Earth hotter.

☐ Children use computers all the time and don't play outside.

☐ People feel lonely because they work with machines, not other people.

☐ People travel a lot and get very tired.

☐ When we throw machines away, we make a lot of rubbish.

 Now compare your answers with your friends.

 Kid's Box Teacher's Resource Book 4   © Cambridge University Press 2015 **PHOTOCOPIABLE**

Reinforcement worksheet 1

- Pupils colour in the adjectives in the wordsearch. They then copy the remaining letters exactly in the same order as they are in the wordsearch to find a joke containing a superlative. Explain the meaning of *sharpest* and *porcupine*. They then complete the table with the superlative form of each of the adjectives.

Key: Question: Which side of a porcupine is the sharpest? Answer: The outside!

1 quiet – the quietest, 2 exciting – the most exciting, 3 loud – the loudest, 4 big – the biggest, 5 heavy – the heaviest, 6 beautiful – the most beautiful, 7 long – the longest, 8 short – the shortest, 9 small – the smallest, 10 good – the best, 11 tall – the tallest, 12 bad – the worst, 13 boring – the most boring, 14 clever – the cleverest.

- *Optional follow-up activity:* Ask pupils to think of the longest city, town or village name they know. Then tell them that the longest town name in the world belongs to a town in Wales called: *Llanfairpwllgwyngyllgogerychwyrndrobwllllantysiliogogogoch.*

The name means 'The church of St Mary in the hollow of white hazel trees near the rapid whirlpool by St Tysilio's of the red cave'.

Reinforcement worksheet 2

- Pupils read the questions in the grid. They find the animals in the picture and write numbers to answer the questions. They then work out the missing numbers by getting each row and each column of the grid to add up to 20. They then write questions for the other five squares in the grid.

Key: Top line: 7, 9 (Which lion is the quietest?), 4 (Which elephant is the heaviest?) Middle line: 2, 8, 10, Bottom line: 11 (Which monkey is the smallest?), 3 (Which monkey is the biggest?), 6 (Which snake is the shortest?). Please note that number 12 is not used.

- *Optional follow-up activity:* In their notebooks, pupils draw a similar grid and write sentences, e.g. *Giraffe number 7 is the tallest.*

Extension worksheet 1

- Pupils read the requirements and decide which animal is best suited to each child. They complete the responses. They choose one of the remaining animals and write about it for a friend to guess. They can write in their notebooks or on the back of the worksheet, as you prefer.

Key: Sally – crocodile, Peter – bat, Vicky – snake, Paul – parrot.

- *Optional follow-up activity:* People say pet owners choose pets that look like them. Pupils choose Sally, Peter, Vicky or Paul and draw him/her to look like his/her animal.

Extension worksheet 2

- Pupils listen to the story (Track 16) and follow on the worksheet. They then follow the instructions to write the sentences from the story. They can write in their notebooks or on the back of the worksheet, as you prefer.

Key: See Pupil's Book, page 69.

- *Optional follow-up activity:* In groups of four, each pupil cuts out the six frames. The dealer shuffles them and deals them all out. Pupil A puts one of the frames face up on the table and the others race to put down the next frame. The first to do so keeps the cards and play passes to Pupil B, and so on. The game continues until one pupil has won all the cards. Tell the pupils that, in this game, frame 1 follows on from frame 6.

Song worksheet

- Pupils put the verbs into the past tense to complete the song. They listen to the song (Track 17) to check their answers. They then draw a picture of themselves and what they did at the zoo.

Key: See Pupil's Book, page 67.

- *Optional follow-up activity:* If pupils have already written a new verse (see Pupil's Book, page 67), make a list of the new animals on the board and, beside each one, the actions the pupils have assigned to them. Vote on the best combinations and then sing the new verse(s). If the pupils have not yet done so, they can make up a new verse at this point.

Topic worksheet

- Pupils first read the text to give them an idea of what numbers might be used for which gap. They then record their guesses with a pencil. They do the maths at the bottom of the page to check their answers.

Key: 1 300, 2 27, 3 3, 4 2, 5 7, 6 27, 7 30, 8 61, 9 54, 10 300, 11 33, 12 9, 13 2, 14 26.

- *Optional follow-up activity:* Pupils think of alternative mathematical operations to give the same numbers. They take it in turns to say the operation and the rest must work out the answer and name the fact(s) from the text to which the number refers.

Reinforcement worksheet 1

Find and colour the adjectives.

| ~~quiet~~ exciting |
| loud   big |
| heavy   beautiful |
| long   short |
| small   good |
| tall   bad |
| boring   clever |

q	b	w	h	i	h	e	a	v	y	b	c
u	h	i	s	i	d	x	e	o	f	o	a
i	p	o	g	r	c	c	u	p	i	r	n
e	b	e	a	u	t	i	f	u	l	i	e
t	i	s	t	h	e	t	s	l	o	n	g
h	s	h	o	r	t	i	a	r	u	g	p
e	s	t	t	h	a	n	e	o	d	u	t
s	g	o	o	d	l	g	s	m	a	l	l
b	a	d	i	c	l	e	v	e	r	d	e

Find the extra letters across (→) the wordsearch. Write them on the lines to find a joke.

Question: W h i _ _   _ _ _ _   _ _   _   _ _ _ _ _ _ _ _ _ _   _ _

_ _ _   _ _ _ _ _ _ _ _ ?

Answer: _ _ _   _ _ _ _ _ _ _ _ !

Complete the table.

Adjective	Superlative form	Adjective	Superlative form
1 quiet	the quietest	8 short	
2 exciting		9 small	
3 loud		10 good	
4 big		11 tall	
5 heavy		12 bad	
6 beautiful		13 boring	
7 long		14 clever	

Unit 7 — Reinforcement worksheet 2

⭐ **Find the animals. Number the questions.**

| biggest | ~~shortest~~ | smallest | heaviest | shortest | quietest |

→ = 20

7 Which giraffe is the tallest?	☐	**4**
☐ Which snake is the longest?	**8** Which giraffe is the shortest?	☐ Which lion is the loudest?
☐	**3** Which	☐

= 20 (left) = 20 (right)

→ = 20

⭐ **Each line → and ↓ = 20. Think and write questions.**

⭐ **Read, think and write.**

I want to buy an animal. I want a reptile but I don't like snakes. I want the most dangerous one that you have.	I like animals that can fly but I'm allergic to feathers. I want the smallest animal that you have.	I live in a flat so I want an animal that doesn't go outside. Mum says I have to have the quietest animal that you have.	I want an animal that lays eggs. I want it to fly and I want it to have the most beautiful feathers.
Sally ₒ○◯	Peter ₒ○◯	Vicky ₒ○◯	Paul ₒ○◯

Dear Sally,

I think the best animal for you is

a .... because

....

....

....

Dear Peter,

I think the best animal for you is

....

....

....

....

Dear Vicky,

I think ....

....

....

....

Dear Paul,

I think ....

....

....

....

Kid's Box Teacher's Resource Book 4   © Cambridge University Press 2015   **PHOTOCOPIABLE**

Unit 7 Extension worksheet 2

Read the clues. Write the sentences from the story.

1. Lock says this when the phone rings.
2. Key asks the zoo keeper this question the first time we see him.
3. The zoo keeper describes this problem when Lock is talking to his motorbike.
4. Lock asks this question when he shows the zoo keeper the picture of Nick Motors.
5. Lock says this when he answers the phone.
6. The person who calls Lock says this to explain why Lock must come quickly.
7. Nick Motors says this when he is in the lorry with the tiger.

Song worksheet

 Change the verbs into the past to complete the song.

The elephants *drink* drank , *drink* _____ , *drink* _____ ,

The parrots *fly* _____ , *fly* _____ , *fly* _____ ,

The dolphins *swim* _____ , *swim* _____ , *swim* _____ ,

At the zoo, zoo, zoo. ... (x 2)

What *do* _____ you do, what *do* _____ you do,

What *do* _____ you do,

When you *see* _____ , *see* _____ , *see* _____ them

At the zoo, zoo, zoo?

The monkeys *eat* _____ , *eat* _____ , *eat* _____ ,

The children *draw* _____ , *draw* _____ , *draw* _____ ,

The lions *sleep* _____ , *sleep* _____ , *sleep* _____ ,

At the zoo, zoo, zoo. ... (x 2)

What *do* _____ you do, what *do* _____ you do,

What *do* _____ you do,

When you *see* _____ , *see* _____ , *see* _____ them

At the zoo, zoo, zoo? ... (x 2)

 17 Listen and check. Sing.

 What did you do at the zoo? Draw a picture.

Kid's Box Teacher's Resource Book 4   © Cambridge University Press 2015   **PHOTOCOPIABLE**

Unit 7

Topic worksheet

 Read about bones in humans and animals.
Guess the correct number each time. Use a pencil!
To check your answers, do the maths at the bottom
of the page.

| 2 | 2 | 3 | 7 | 9 | 26 | 27 | 27 | 30 |
| 33 | 54 | 61 | ~~206~~ | 300 | 300 |

There are ...206... bones in the human body but babies have about (1) .... bones because not all the bones are joined. They 'fuse', or join, when the baby is older.

There are (2) .... bones in each hand. About half these are in the round part of your hand but there are (3) .... bones in each finger and (4) .... bones in each thumb. Can you find them?

All mammals have (5) .... neck bones, which means that you have the same number of bones in your neck as a giraffe!

The bones in your back are called vertebrae. All dogs have (6) .... vertebrae up to the start of the tail but different dogs have different numbers of bones in their tails.

A cat has (7) .... vertebrae, an elephant has (8) .... , a horse has (9) .... and some snakes have (10) .... ! Humans are born with (11) .... but (12) .... of these fuse into (13) .... so then there are (14) ....

Answers

1 100 + 100 + 100 =   4 6 ÷ 3 =   7 10 × 3 =   10 400 − 100 =   13 10 ÷ 5 =

2 9 × 3 =   5 4 + 3 =   8 36 + 25 =   11 27 + 6 =   14 28 − 2 =

3 10 − 7 =   6 30 − 3 =   9 6 × 9 =   12 3 × 3 =

8 Teacher's notes

Reinforcement worksheet 1

- Pupils follow the drawing instructions. Elicit words they know for food and things in the kitchen. Ask what shape they have drawn (a bowl). They then complete the text at the bottom of the worksheet.

Key: bottle – cup, sandwiches – soup, vegetables – cheese, pasta – bottle, glass – box, vegetables – soup, sandwiches – salad, salad – pasta, cup – glass, box – cheese.

- *Optional follow-up activity:* Pupils think of a different shape/route and write the instructions for another member of class.

Reinforcement worksheet 2

- Pupils follow the example to write sentences about the pictures using the *want … to do* structure. They then do the named activities noting the words they think of and the time taken. They can time each other in pairs for the counting and spelling activities.

Key: 2 The teacher wants the children to count from 50 to 1 in English.
3 The teacher wants the children to draw a house with five windows.
4 The teacher wants the children to spell the name of the school in English.
5 The teacher wants the children to write two words which rhyme with 'cat'.
6 The teacher wants the children to write four different fruit.

- *Optional follow-up activity:* In groups of four, pupils take it in turns to say, e.g. *I took (amount of time) to (action)*. When they have all said their sentences, Pupil A says, e.g. *Maria sang the song most quickly*. For the next action, Pupil B has to say who did the action most quickly, etc.

Extension worksheet 1

- Pupils write the story with *want(s) … to do* sentences.

Key: 2 He wants Dad to buy a ball.
3 Tom's dad doesn't want him/Tom to swim in the lake.
4 Tom wants the dog to get the ball.

- *Optional follow-up activity:* Pupils think of a title and write the dialogue to turn the story into a short play.

Extension worksheet 2

- This can be done as a listening exercise (Track 18) or a reading exercise. If you use the audio recording, pause after each frame while the pupils write. Pupils find the words in the story and replace them with their opposites to correct the story text.

Key: See Pupil's Book, page 77.

- *Optional follow-up activity:* In groups of four, pupils agree on a way to describe each frame, for example, *The picture where Lock is …* Each pupil cuts out the six frames. The dealer shuffles them and deals three to each pupil. The rest are put in a pile in the middle. Pupils look at their own cards but do not show them to the group. Pupil A asks another pupil for a card using the description on which they have agreed. If the pupil has it, he/she must hand it over. Once a player has two frames the same, he/she puts them aside. If he/she does not have it, Pupil A has to pick up one of the cards from the pile. Play continues round the circle. The winner is the player with the most pairs at the end of the game.

Song worksheet

- Pupils replace the underlined words with the correct rhyming words to complete the song. They listen to the song (Track 19) to check their answers.

Key: See Pupil's Book, page 75.

- *Optional follow-up activity:* In groups, pupils think of as many words as possible to rhyme with the words they have paired.

Topic worksheet

- Pupils read about digestion and complete the activity.

Key: 1 bread – chicken – cheese, 2 pasta – fish – butter, 3 rice – eggs – oil.

- *Optional follow-up activity:* Pupils use the second paragraph of the text to work out the longest time a meal is in the body.

Key: Two days, seven hours and forty seconds.

Reinforcement worksheet 1

 Follow the instructions.

When you buy lemonade, it comes in this. Start here and draw a line to the thing that you use to drink hot drinks.

When you have a picnic, you normally eat these. Draw a line from them to the hot liquid that you eat with a spoon.

Some children say that they don't like these. Draw a line from them to the food made from milk.

Draw a line from the food that comes from Italy to the thing that you buy lemonade in.

You use this to drink cold drinks. Draw a line from it to the thing you use to carry a lot of bottles.

Draw a line from the food that some children don't like to the hot liquid that you eat with a spoon.

Draw a line from the food that you normally eat on a picnic to the food that you eat cold with meat.

Draw a line from the food that you eat cold with meat to the food from Italy.

Draw a line from the thing you use to drink hot drinks to the thing you use to drink cold drinks.

Draw a line from the thing you use to carry a lot of bottles to the food made from milk.

 Complete the text.

I drew a line from the bottle to the cup, from the _____

_____

_____ and from the box to the cheese.

© Cambridge University Press 2015   Kid's Box Teacher's Resource Book 4

Reinforcement worksheet 2

 Write sentences about the pictures.

> Please write five words beginning with 'p'.

1 The teacher wants the children to write five words beginning with 'p'.

> Please count from 50 to 1 in English.

2 The teacher wants

> Please draw a house with five windows.

3 The teacher

> Please spell the name of the school in English.

4 The teacher

> Please write two words which rhyme with 'cat'.

5 The teacher

> Please write four different fruit.

6 The teacher

 Do the activities. How long do you take?

1 Words beginning with 'p': ... I took ... seconds.

Extension worksheet 1

Write the story. Use 'want ... to' (✓) or 'doesn't want ... to' (✗) and these words.

✗ ~~dog / play with him~~   ✓ Dad / buy / ball   ✗ swim / lake   ✓ get / ball

1 Tom *doesn't want the dog to play with him.*

2 He _____

_____

3 Tom's dad _____

_____

4 Tom _____

_____

© Cambridge University Press 2015   Kid's Box Teacher's Resource Book 4

Extension worksheet 2

Find the words in the story. Cross them out and write the opposite.

~~here~~   We haven't got   that   horrible   Don't have
women   no thank you   can   didn't catch   Yes?

there

Kid's Box Teacher's Resource Book 4   © Cambridge University Press 2015

PHOTOCOPIABLE

Unit 8 Song worksheet

 The <u>underlined</u> words are wrong. Correct them with words that rhyme.

We <u>bad</u> ......had...... soup,

He .... had pasta,

We had salads and <u>please</u> ....

We all wanted <u>four</u> .... ,

We all <u>red</u> .... 'please'.

We <u>wave</u> .... presents,

<u>Sand</u> .... cards which we <u>played</u>

....

We <u>more</u> .... fancy dress,

We danced and we <u>made</u> ....

The party was <u>could</u> .... ,

The party was <u>eight</u> ....

And now it's time to fly.

The party was <u>could</u> .... ,

The party was <u>eight</u> ....

We'll see you <u>moon</u> .... ,

Goodbye.

The drinks we <u>bank</u> .... ,

The food <u>she</u> .... ate.

The party was <u>could</u> .... ,

The party was <u>eight</u> ....

We <u>wave</u> .... presents ...

<u>How</u> .... the party's over,

Now it's time to <u>buy</u> ....

See you <u>moon</u> .... ,

Goodbye.

 🔊19 Listen and check. Sing.

Unit 8 Topic worksheet

 Read about digestion.

What is digestion?

Our body needs to break our food down so that we can use it. This is called digestion. Digestion begins in the mouth. Our teeth cut the food into smaller and smaller pieces and then the tongue pushes the food to the back of the mouth. It goes down a tube called the oesophagus and into the stomach. In the stomach there are acids which break the food down more. Next the food moves into the small intestine, where the body takes the nutrients from our food. The body takes what it needs from what we eat and the rest goes into the large intestine and leaves the body.

How long does it take?

Our teeth take between five and thirty seconds to cut our food. It then takes ten seconds to travel down the oesophagus. The food is in our stomach for between three and four hours and then in the small intestine for three hours. Finally, it is in the large intestine for between eighteen hours and ... two days!

 DO YOU KNOW THAT ...?

Carbohydrates are in the stomach for the shortest time. Proteins are in the stomach longer and fats are there the longest.

 Write these foods in order depending on the time they spend in the stomach.

1 | cheese   bread   chicken

Shortest time ←——→ Longest time

....cheese........

2 | butter   fish   pasta

Shortest time ←——→ Longest time

....

3 | eggs   rice   oil

Shortest time ←——→ Longest time

....

Kid's Box Teacher's Resource Book 4   © Cambridge University Press 2015   **PHOTOCOPIABLE**

 **Festivals**

Halloween

- Halloween is celebrated on 31 October in the United Kingdom, the United States, Canada, Australia, New Zealand and many other countries around the world.

  It is not a public holiday in the United Kingdom, however it is a very important celebration for children. The word Halloween originally came from *All Hallows' Eve*, which means the evening before the Day of the Holy Ones or All Saints' Day, 1 November. The tradition is that, on this night, spirits, ghosts and witches wander the Earth. People used to make lanterns out of pumpkins and place them in the window to scare away these frightening creatures.

- Nowadays, on the night of Halloween, children get dressed up as witches, ghosts, vampires and other scary monsters, and have a fancy dress party. Items that are traditionally associated with Halloween are pumpkin lanterns, bats, spiders and black cats. Children often play a traditional game called apple bobbing. In this game, you have to bite an apple that is floating in water or hanging on a string. Typical party food would be cakes and pizza decorated with horrible faces.

- At Halloween, children love to play *Trick or Treat*. They knock on neighbours' doors and ask *Trick or Treat?* If the neighbour chooses a treat, he/she must offer the children sweets, chocolate or fruit. If not, the children will play a naughty trick, like using a water pistol! It's always a good idea to have treats ready for visitors at Halloween!

Halloween worksheet 1

- The figure 3 in the smaller game on the worksheet is an example. Go through the example with the class before pupils play in groups. Pupils decide on an odd number and write it in the middle square. They start counting that number round from the word *Start*, only counting the text sections and not counting *Start/Finish*. Each time they land on a text section, they cross it out. They continue to do this, counting the crossed-out words as well, until they have only one section left on each side. They then use these four elements to write a Halloween sentence.

- *Optional follow-up activity:* Play this at a whole-class level and help the pupils elaborate the sentence into a longer text.

Halloween worksheet 2

- Pupils colour the four pictures then cut out the long strips. They glue or staple the strips together down the black strip, making sure that the dividing lines coincide. They then cut along the horizontal lines of the pictures stopping before the black strip. By turning the different pages of the book, they invent new Halloween characters. They invent a name for their characters. You could also ask them to write sentences to describe them.

- *Optional follow-up activity:* Pupil A folds the pages to make up a character without showing Pupil B. He/She describes it, and Pupil B must make up the same character. They swap roles.

Christmas

- Christmas Day is celebrated in countries around the world on 25 December, to commemorate the birth of Jesus. In the weeks before Christmas, people decorate a Christmas tree with ornaments. They usually put a star on the top to remind them of the story of the birth of Jesus, and the visit of the Three Wise Men. People also like to send each other Christmas cards with typical Christmas scenes and a Christmas message. Younger children write a letter to Father Christmas, or Santa Claus as he is sometimes called, to tell him what they would like for Christmas.

- On Christmas Eve, 24 December, they hang a Christmas stocking at the end of their bed or by the fireplace, if they have one. Traditionally Father Christmas arrives in his sleigh pulled by reindeer. He flies through the air, lands on the roofs of children's houses and delivers the presents by climbing down the chimneys with a huge sack of presents!

- On Christmas Day, families come together to eat a traditional midday meal. This consists of roast turkey, with vegetables. Dessert is a rich fruit pudding served with a brandy sauce that is set alight! The table is decorated with candles and brightly coloured crackers. Everyone pulls the crackers, which make a loud bang. Children love to look inside the crackers to find a colourful paper Christmas hat, a small toy and a Christmas joke.

Christmas worksheet 1

- It is best to photocopy this worksheet onto coloured card. Pupils follow the instructions to make a Christmas card.

- *Optional follow-up activity:* In groups, Pupil A says e.g. *Under the Christmas tree, there was a red present.* Pupil B says, *Under the Christmas tree, there was a red present and a yellow present.* The game continues until one pupil cannot remember the order of the colours. If they manage to say all the colours they know, they can make it more challenging by combining colours, e.g. *a red and yellow present.*

Christmas worksheet 2

- Pupils look at the two pictures and write sentences about the differences.

Key: A angel/fairy **B** star, **A** snowing/day **B** night, **A** three stockings **B** four stockings, **A** Father Christmas **B** a fire, **A** biscuits **B** cake, **A** three presents **B** four presents, **A** milk and one glass **B** water and two glasses, **A** two crackers **B** three crackers.

- *Optional follow-up activity:* In groups, Pupil A says e.g. *In A, we can see three presents under the tree but* … and Pupil B completes the sentence. He/She then begins another sentence for Pupil C to continue. This continues until all the pupils have started and finished a sentence.

Easter

- Easter celebrates the resurrection of Jesus in the Christian religion. Easter Sunday always falls in spring. However, the date is fixed according to the lunar calendar and therefore differs slightly every year. In the weeks before Easter, people send Easter cards to friends and family, and they buy chocolate Easter eggs and Easter bunnies for their children. Many children like to boil real eggs and then paint them with bright colours. Children often have egg-rolling competitions or hold Easter egg hunts with the colourful eggs. Easter baskets are associated with Easter. People fill them with Easter eggs and spring flowers to decorate their houses.

- In the United Kingdom, people like to eat hot cross buns, a type of sweet bread with dried fruit in it. These buns are marked with the Christian symbol of the cross and are traditionally eaten during Lent (the 40 days leading up to Easter). In the Middle Ages, the bakers sold these buns in the streets.

- Easter is an important church festival and Good Friday and Easter Monday are public holidays.

Easter worksheet 1

- Pupils read the text, then decorate the egg using whichever technique they wish (paint, collage, crayons, etc.). Encourage them to be as creative as possible.

- *Optional follow-up activity:* Divide the class into two teams and ask them to prepare a treasure hunt with the eggs. On the back of each egg, they write their name (so that they can take it home afterwards) and an instruction to find the next egg, e.g. *Look by the door.* In one lesson, one team hides the eggs and the pupils in the other team take it in turns to find each egg. In another lesson, the roles can be swapped.
  Ask another teacher to stay with the pupils who will be looking for the eggs, or use break time to hide the eggs so that the teams can't see where they are being hidden.

Easter worksheet 2

- Pupils complete the biscuit recipe. They can mount the chick on card and use it as a biscuit cutter.

Key: 2 butter, 3 bowl, 4 sugar, 5 flour, 6 rolling pin, 7 biscuit cutter, 8 baking tray, 9 oven.

- *Optional follow-up activity:* Ask pupils to find a typical Easter recipe from their country. Help them to translate it into English.

Halloween worksheet 1

 Make and play a game.

It was **a stormy night**. I was in **a castle**.
I saw **a vampire**. I **shouted, 'Aaagh!'**

Start / Finish	midnight	middle of the night	winter	a stormy night	→
shouted, 'Aaagh!'					a haunted house
shouted, 'Help!'					a tunnel
laughed					a castle
ran away					a cave
↑	a witch	a monster	a vampire	a ghost	↘

Kid's Box Teacher's Resource Book 4   © Cambridge University Press 2015   **PHOTOCOPIABLE**

Halloween worksheet 2

 Make a book. Invent a new character.

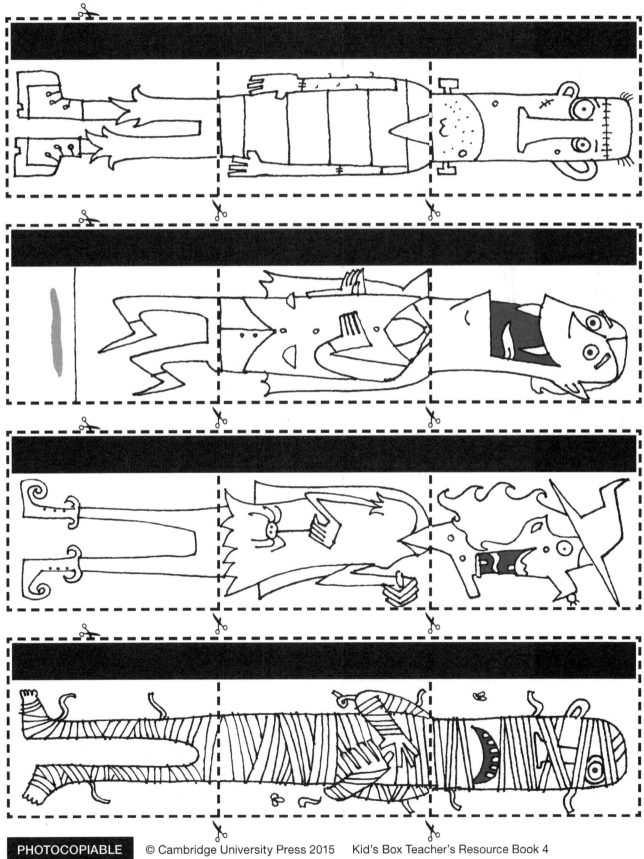

Christmas worksheet 1

 Make a card.

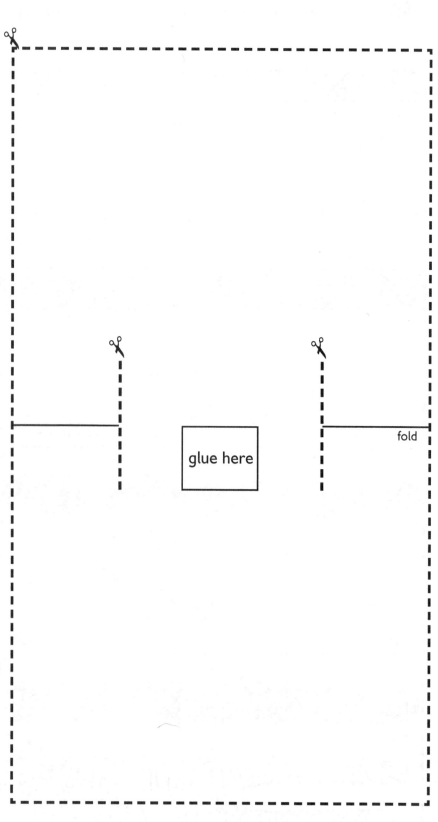

glue here

fold

- Colour and decorate the tree.
- Cut it out.
- Cut along the dotted lines.
- Fold along the solid line.
- Push the centre section forward.
- Glue the tree to the card.
- Close it.
- Write 'Happy Christmas' on the front.

Christmas worksheet 2

 Spot the differences.

In A, there are baubles on the tree. In B, there are candles.

© Cambridge University Press 2015   Kid's Box Teacher's Resource Book 4

Easter worksheet 1

 Read about eggs. Decorate the egg.

Eggs are a symbol of the universe and of rebirth. The Romans, in their spring festivals, gave each other eggs, which they decorated. Christians associate eggs with the resurrection so they give each other eggs at Easter. In medieval times, rich people decorated eggs with gold to give as presents but other people decorated them by boiling them with plants, leaves or insects. This changed the colour.

The ostrich lays the biggest eggs. They are 15 cm long and weigh 1.4 kg. The humming bird lays the smallest eggs. They are 1 cm long and weigh 0.35g.

In the United Kingdom, people eat an average of 170 eggs per year: 140 as eggs and 30 as an ingredient of other food.

Put an egg in water. A fresh egg *sinks* to the bottom and lies on its side. A very old egg *floats* at the top.

The emu lays dark green eggs that then turn black!

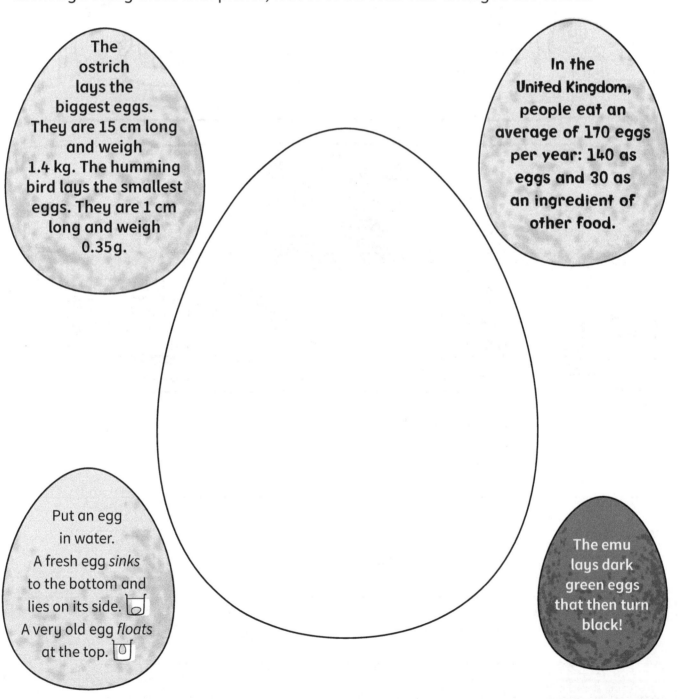

Kid's Box Teacher's Resource Book 4 © Cambridge University Press 2015 **PHOTOCOPIABLE**

Easter worksheet 2

 Complete the recipe with these words.

sugar   rolling pin   ~~spoon~~   oven   baking tray

butter   flour   biscuit cutter   bowl

Ingredients
125 g butter
50 g sugar
175 g flour

Use a wooden [1] __spoon__ to make the [2] _____ soft in a [3] _____ .

Add the [4] _____ . Mix.

Add the [5] _____ . Knead.

Use a [6] _____ to roll out the dough.

Use the [7] _____ to make the shapes. Put them on a [8] _____ .

Bake in the [9] _____ at 150°C for 25 minutes. Cool.

 Put the chick onto card to make a biscuit cutter. Make Easter biscuits.

Word cards: Back to school

boring

busy

careful

difficult

easy

exciting

quick

slow

terrible

Kid's Box Teacher's Resource Book 4 Word cards   © Cambridge University Press 2015

PHOTOCOPIABLE

Word cards: Good sports

inside

outside

fish

dance

sail

skate

climb

run

skip

swim

Word cards: Health matters

ate

drank

gave

had

saw

took

was

went

were

Word cards: After school club

first	eleventh
second	twelfth
third	thirteenth
fourth	fourteenth
fifth	fifteenth
sixth	sixteenth
seventh	seventeenth
eighth	eighteenth
ninth	nineteenth
tenth	twentieth

Word cards: Exploring our world

caught

found

got

made

could

lost

came

Word cards: Technology

bought

chose

knew

put

read

said

thought

Word cards: At the zoo

round	next to
behind	on
between	opposite
in	out of
in front of	under
into	

Kid's Box Teacher's Resource Book 4 Word cards

Word cards: Let's party!

bottle	pasta
bowl	salad
cheese	sandwich
coffee	soup
cup	tea
fruit	vegetables
glass	

Word cards: numbers (1)

12	twelve	**20**	twenty
13	thirteen	**30**	thirty
14	fourteen	**40**	forty
15	fifteen	**50**	fifty
16	sixteen	**60**	sixty
17	seventeen	**70**	seventy
18	eighteen	**80**	eighty
19	nineteen	**90**	ninety

 Kid's Box Teacher's Resource Book 4 Word cards © Cambridge University Press 2015

Word cards: numbers (2)

11	eleven
22	twenty-two
33	thirty-three
44	forty-four
55	fifty-five
66	sixty-six
77	seventy-seven
88	eighty-eight
99	ninety-nine
100	a hundred

Name: ....

Class: ....

 Listen and draw lines. There is one example.

Paul   John   Vicky   Daisy

Jane   Jim   Mary

2 🔊 **Listen and write. There is one example.**

THE LIBRARY

	Name:	Sally ......Brown......
1	How old?	....
2	School:	.... School
3	Teacher's name:	Mrs ....
4	Favourite author:	.... Wilson
5	Favourite book:	....

3 🔵22 **What did Paul do last week?**

Listen and draw a line from the day to the correct picture. There is one example.

Monday

Tuesday

Wednesday

Thursday

Friday

Saturday

Sunday

Kid's Box TRB 4   Test Units 1–4   p3 Listening   © Cambridge University Press 2015

PHOTOCOPIABLE

4 ㉓ **Listen and tick (✓) the box. There is one example.**

What was the matter with Jim?

A ☐

B ☐

C ✓

1 Which is the doctor?

A ☐

B ☐

C ☐

2 Where did Jim go on Friday?

A ☐

B ☐

C ☐

3 What does Jim like best?

 **A** ☐

 **B** ☐

 **C** ☐

4 How old is Jim's sister?

 **A** ☐

 **B** ☐

 **C** ☐

5 How many books did she have for her birthday?

 **A** ☐

 **B** ☐

 **C** ☐

Listen and colour and write. There is one example.

Name: ....

Class: ....

 Look and read. Choose the correct words and write them on the lines. There is one example.

a doctor

a moustache

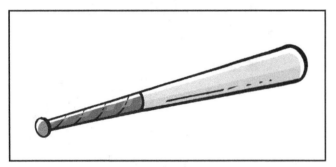

a bat

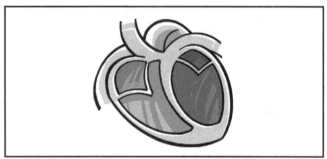

the heart

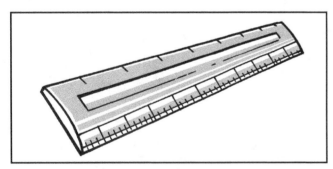

a ruler

glasses

a beard

a boat

Example

This moves blood around our body. ....the heart..........

Questions

1 People who can't see very well wear these.

....

2 Some men have this on their face between their nose and their mouth.

....

3 You use this to measure length.

....

4 You sail in this.

....

5 You use this to hit the ball in baseball.

....

6 This person helps you when you are ill.

....

2 **Look and read. Write yes or no.**

Examples

The teacher with a beard is talking to a boy.	.............yes.............
Four windows are open.	.............no.............

Questions

1 A girl is hopping carefully. ----------------------------

2 The boy with a cap is playing football. ----------------------------

3 There is a tree behind the school. ----------------------------

4 The teacher with glasses is carrying a bag. ----------------------------

5 The girl with short hair is wearing a skirt. ----------------------------

6 A girl and a boy are reading. ----------------------------

3 Read the text and choose the best answer.
Sally is talking to her friend Mary.

Example

Sally:	Hello, Mary. How are you?
Mary:	A I'm your friend.
	(B) I'm fine, thanks.
	C I'm slow.

Questions

1 Sally: What are you doing?

Mary: A I'm going to my dance class.

B I go to my dance class.

C I went to my dance class.

2 Sally: Where is the dance class?

  Mary: A I like dancing.

    B At school.

    C At six o'clock.

3 Sally: Do you go every Thursday?

  Mary: A Yes, and Tuesdays, too.

    B I went on Thursday.

    C I'm going on Thursday.

4 Sally: Do you like dancing?

  Mary: A Yes, I like.

    B Yes, please.

    C Yes, I do.

5 Sally: Why do you like dancing?

  Mary: A It's terrible.

    B It's exciting.

    C When I was little.

6 Sally: You must go now. See you!

  Mary: A Yes, I can see you.

    B Where are you?

    C Goodbye.

4 Read the story. Choose a word from the box. Write the correct word next to numbers 1–6. There is one example.

My name is Paul. I am a teacher at a ...sports centre.... . I teach badminton,

1 .... , baseball and running. Yesterday, a new

2 .... came to the class for the first time. When we

played baseball, she hit the **3** .... very hard and she

4 .... very quickly. We couldn't find the ball and her team

won the game. Her team was very **5** .... The next

6 .... we played, I took lots of balls so we could play

all the time.

sad

tennis

ran

ball

sports centre

day

girl

happy

boy

7 **Now choose the best name for the story. Tick one box.**

The baseball game ☐

The tennis class ☐

A game that Paul couldn't play ☐

5 **Look at the pictures and read the story. Write some words to complete the sentences about the story. You can use 1, 2 or 3 words.**

Sam, the teacher!

Sam lives in the countryside with his parents and his sister, Mary, and his brother, Paul. Sam is ten, Mary is eight and Paul is six. They live in the countryside but they go to school in the city. Sam is the one who likes Science, his sister is the one who likes Sport and his brother is the one who likes Art.

Examples

Sam's family ....*live in the*........ countryside.

Sam has a ....*sister*........ called Mary.

Questions

1 The children go to school ....

2 Sam's favourite subject is ....

3 .... is the one who likes Sport.

Last week, Sam had a class about the human body. He listened carefully and when he went home he gave his younger brother and sister a class about the subject. They wanted to listen because it was very interesting. Sam said, 'We move because we have 600 muscles in our body. The muscles need oxygen. We use our lungs to take oxygen from the air into our body.'

4 Last week, Sam studied _____ at school.

5 Sam gave his brother and sister a class when he went

_____ .

6 Mary and Paul wanted to learn because it was very

_____ .

7 We use our lungs because our muscles _____ .

Sam showed his brother and sister how to test their lungs. They took a balloon. First, Sam breathed into the balloon and measured it with the air in. Mary was second and Paul was third. Sam's balloon was bigger than Mary's and Mary's was bigger than Paul's. Now Mary and Paul think that Science is exciting, too.

8 The children used _____ to test their lungs.

9 First the children breathed into the balloons and then they _____ them.

10 Sam's brother and sister think that _____ is exciting.

Blank page

6 Read the text. Choose the right words and write them on the lines.

Football

Example	**You play football ⎯⎯on⎯⎯ a field with a big white**
❶	ball called a football. There ⎯⎯⎯⎯ two teams with
❷	eleven players. Both teams try to score goals ⎯⎯⎯⎯
	kicking or heading the ball into the other team's goal.
❸	Players can use ⎯⎯⎯⎯ feet, head, legs and chest to touch
	the ball but only the goalkeeper can use his or her hands
	and arms. The winning team is the team with more goals
❹	⎯⎯⎯⎯ 90 minutes. People play football all over the world
❺	and the ⎯⎯⎯⎯ football World Cup was in Uruguay
	in 1930.

Example on   in   at

1   are   is   were

2   from   by   to

3   his   your   their

4   after   before   into

5   first   last   next

Find the Differences

Picture Story

Odd-One-Out

Name: _____

Class: _____

 Listen and draw lines. There is one example.

May   Anna   Fred   John

Paul   Kim   Daisy

2 **26** **Listen and write. There is one example.**

MY PARTY

	When?	Friday
1	How many friends?	
2	John's age on Friday:	
3	Favourite food:	
4	How many bottles of water?	
5	Name of film:	

     Kid's Box TRB 4   Test Units 5–8   p2 Listening   © Cambridge University Press 2015   **PHOTOCOPIABLE**

3 🔘 What did Sally do last week?

Listen and draw a line from the day to the correct picture. There is one example.

Monday

Tuesday

Wednesday

Thursday

Friday

Saturday

Sunday

28 **Listen and tick (✓) the box. There is one example.**

Where did Jack go?

A ✓

B ☐

C ☐

1 What did Jack's parents buy him?

A ☐

B ☐

C ☐

2 What did their parents buy for Jack's sister?

A ☐

B ☐

C ☐

Kid's Box TRB 4   Test Units 5–8   p4 Listening   © Cambridge University Press 2015

3 What animals did Jack take photos of?

A ☐

B ☐

C ☐

4 What did they eat at the zoo?

A ☐

B ☐

C ☐

5 What toy animal did Jack buy?

A ☐

B ☐

C ☐

5 🔊 **Listen and colour and draw. There is one example.**

Kid's Box TRB 4   Test Units 5–8   p6 Listening   © Cambridge University Press 2015   **PHOTOCOPIABLE**

Blank page

Name: ···

Class: ···

 Look and read. Choose the correct words and write them on the lines. There is one example.

a pen

a giraffe

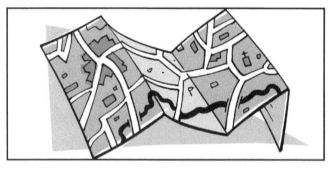

a map

a polar bear

a camera

a button

a dolphin

a forest

Example

This animal is a mammal that lives in the sea.   ....a dolphin...........

Questions

1 You use this to help you when you are lost.   ---------------------------

2 This is lots of trees.   ---------------------------

3 This tall animal lives in hot countries.
It has a very long neck.   ---------------------------

4 You press this to put the radio on or off.   ---------------------------

5 You use this to write with.   ---------------------------

6 You take photos with this.   ---------------------------

2 Look and read. Write **yes** or **no**.

Examples

There is a lot of food on the table.   yes

All the children are wearing fancy dress.   no

Questions

1 The plate of sandwiches is bigger than the plate of biscuits.

----

2 The nurse and the clown are crying.

----

3 All the children are playing a game.

----

4 There are seven presents.

----

5 There are five glasses on the table.

----

6 The tallest girl is dancing.

Read the text and choose the best answer.
Jack is talking to his friend Daisy.

Example

Jack: Hello, Daisy. What's the matter?

Daisy: A What's the matter?

(B) My mobile phone isn't working.

C Yes, it is.

Questions

❶ Jack: Do you usually use the phone a lot?

Daisy: A No, I don't use.

B Yes, every day.

C Yes, I use.

2 Jack: Do you want to buy a new one?

Daisy: A Yes, I want.

B No, I don't want.

C Yes, I'd like to buy one.

3 Jack: Shall I come with you?

Daisy: A I'd like that, thanks.

B He can come.

C I can come tomorrow.

4 Jack: Do you want the phone to take photos?

Daisy: A No, it doesn't.

B Yes, I do.

C He wants photos.

5 Jack: What colour phone do you want?

Daisy: A Black or blue.

B No, thank you.

C Yes, it does.

6 Jack: Do you like texting your friends?

Daisy: A Yes, they do.

B Yes, I like my friends.

C Yes, a lot.

4 Read the story. Choose a word from the box. Write the correct word next to numbers 1–6. There is one example.

My dad works in a hospital. He's a ....doctor........ . Yesterday, it was his

birthday but in the **1** .... , we didn't say 'Happy Birthday'

and there weren't any **2** .... Dad came home at

3 .... o'clock. The house was very quiet. My family and

Dad's friends were in the **4** .... Dad opened the door and

we **5** .... 'Happy Birthday!' Dad was very surprised! We ate

a lot of **6** .... and had a great time.

living room

teacher

food

morning

shouted

six

drinks

presents

doctor

7 **Now choose the best name for the story. Tick one box.**

A day in the hospital ☐

Dad's party ☐

At home with my family ☐

5 Look at the pictures and read the story. Write some words to complete the sentences about the story. You can use 1, 2 or 3 words.

Visiting Grandma and Grandpa

Last week, Vicky and her brothers, Paul and Peter, visited their grandparents. Paul is older than Vicky and Vicky is older than Peter. They like visiting their grandparents because they tell the children lots of stories. On Thursday, they went to the cinema and their grandfather said that when they made the first films, you couldn't hear the actors speak. People watched the actors and read the story. Someone played the piano because the machine that showed the films was very noisy.

Examples

Vicky ...has two brothers... who are called Peter and Paul.

Paul is the ....oldest.......... .

Questions

1 Vicky's grandparents know lots of _____ .

2 In the past, people had to _____ the story when they watched a film.

3 Music on _____ covered the noise of the machine.

On Friday, it was sunny so they went to the zoo. They took photos of the animals. The giraffes were the tallest animals and the elephants were the heaviest but the monkeys were the funniest.

4 The family went to the zoo because _____ .

5 The giraffes were _____ than the other animals.

6 The monkeys were _____ animals.

→

After the zoo, they went home. When Vicky's grandparents were young, they went on a safari. They showed the children photos of the animals that they saw in Africa. The photos were in black and white. The boys' favourite was a photo of a giraffe drinking water but Vicky's favourite was of an elephant and her baby. The baby elephant was heavier than Vicky!

7 They went home _____ the zoo.

8 They saw _____ photos of animals in Africa.

9 The boys liked the photo of a giraffe _____ .

10 The baby elephant weighed more _____ Vicky.

6 Read the text. Choose the right words and write them on the lines.

Pandas

Example	Pandas belong to the bear family. They come ____from____ the
1	south of China and they live _____ bamboo forests in the
	mountains. They have the digestive system of carnivores but
2	99% of what they _____ is bamboo. They also eat eggs,
	fish, oranges and bananas. They eat 10–15 kg of bamboo
3	_____ day to have enough energy. Their fingers are
4	strong to hold the bamboo. When they _____ born they
	are the size of a mouse. They weigh 90–130 g but when
5	they are adults they are a lot bigger. They _____ weigh
	100–150 kg! They can climb trees well.

Example	to	from	of
1	in	on	under
2	eating	eat	eats
3	every	most	what
4	were	aren't	are
5	don't	can	is

Find the Differences

Picture Story

Kid's Box TRB 4   Test Units 5–8   p21 Speaking   © Cambridge University Press 2015   **PHOTOCOPIABLE**

Odd-One-Out

© Cambridge University Press 2015   p22 Speaking   Test Units 5–8   Kid's Box TRB 4

Marks are not shown on the Tests themselves
to allow you the flexibility to mark in a way that suits your
teaching situation. However, a suggested scheme is given
below which you may wish to use. This scheme gives a total
of 85 marks for each test. Note that all four skills carry equal
weight in the Cambridge ESOL YLE Tests. There are two
complete tests in this section.

Marking Key

( ) = Acceptable extra words are placed in brackets.
/ = A single slash is placed between acceptable alternative
words within an answer.
// = A double slash is placed between acceptable alternative
complete answers.

Test Units 1–4 pp 90–112

Page 1: Listening Part 1 (5 marks)

Key: Lines should be drawn between:
1 John and front boy in swimming race
2 Jane and girl skating and wearing jeans
3 Mary and girl sitting under tree
4 Jim and boy climbing and wearing black hat
5 Vicky and girl with badminton racket and wearing
white hat

TRACK 20

HEADING: *Look at the picture. Listen and look.
There is one example.*
WOMAN: Excuse me. What are you doing?
GIRL: We're learning different sports.
WOMAN: Who's your teacher?
GIRL: The woman standing by the swimming pool.
WOMAN: The tall one?
GIRL: That's right. Her name's Daisy.

HEADING: *Can you see the line? This is an example.
Now you listen and draw lines.*
1
WOMAN: Who's the boy who's swimming?
GIRL: Which one?
WOMAN: The one who's first.
GIRL: That's John. He swims very quickly.
WOMAN: Yes, he swims very well.
2
GIRL: Can you see the girl who's skating?
WOMAN: The one wearing jeans?
GIRL: Yes. She's my friend, Jane.
WOMAN: How old is she?
GIRL: Ten, like me.
3
WOMAN: Who's the girl who's sitting under the tree?
GIRL: That's Mary. She isn't very well. She had a temperature
yesterday.
WOMAN: It's good that she's not in the sun.
GIRL: I know.

4
WOMAN: Who's the boy with the black hat?
GIRL: The one who's climbing?
WOMAN: That's right. He's careful. He's wearing a strong hat.
GIRL: That's my brother, Jim.
5
WOMAN: And the girl with the white hat. Who's she?
GIRL: She's Vicky. She plays badminton very well.
WOMAN: Do you like badminton?
GIRL: Yes, I do, but I think it's a bit difficult.

HEADING: *Now listen again.*
(The tapescript is repeated.)

Page 2: Listening Part 2 (5 marks)
Key: 1 10//ten, 2 City, 3 Smith, 4 Vicky, 5 Quickly.

TRACK 21

HEADING: *Listen and look. There is one example.*
MAN: Hello. Are you here to visit the library?
GIRL: Yes.
MAN: OK. Can I ask you some questions first, please?
GIRL: Of course.
MAN: What's your name?
GIRL: Sally Brown.
MAN: Is that B R O W N?
GIRL: That's right.

HEADING: *Can you see the answer? Now you listen
and write.*
1
MAN: Are you nine or ten, Sally?
GIRL: I'm ten. It's my birthday today.
MAN: Really? Happy Birthday!
GIRL: Thank you.
2
MAN: Are you here with your school?
GIRL: Yes, that's right.
MAN: What's the name of your school?
GIRL: It's City School.
MAN: Oh yes. City School is near here, isn't it?
GIRL: That's right.
3
MAN: Is that your teacher over there?
GIRL: Yes, that's Mrs Smith.
MAN: Mrs Smith. S M I T H.
GIRL: She loves books and we love reading.
MAN: That's very good.
4
MAN: You say you love reading.
GIRL: That's right.
MAN: Do you have a favourite author?
GIRL: Yes, I think Vicky Wilson is great.
MAN: I like Vicky Wilson's books, too.
5
MAN: Do you have a favourite book?
GIRL: It's difficult to choose. I think *Picnic in the Countryside* is
very funny but *Quickly* is very exciting. Yes, I think *Quickly*
is my favourite.

MAN: Thank you very much. Goodbye.
GIRL: Goodbye.

HEADING: *Now listen again.*
(The tapescript is repeated.)

Page 3: Listening Part 3 (5 marks)

Key:

Tuesday (example)	Saturday
Friday	Monday
Wednesday	Thursday

TRACK 22

HEADING: *Look at the pictures. What did Paul do last week? Listen and look. There is one example.*
MAN: Hello, Paul. You're very brown.
BOY: Yes. I was on holiday last week.
MAN: That's nice. Was it sunny every day?
BOY: Well, on Tuesday it rained so we went to the cinema and saw a film about monkeys.
MAN: Who did you go with?
BOY: My parents and my brother.

HEADING: *Can you see the line from the word Tuesday? On Tuesday, Paul saw a film about monkeys. Now you listen and draw lines.*
1
MAN: Do you like going to the cinema?
BOY: Yes, I went on Friday, too, but this time with my friends.
MAN: Did you see the same film?
BOY: No, we saw a film about cars. It was great.
MAN: Oh yes. I know the film. It's very exciting.
2
MAN: What did you do on Wednesday?
BOY: We went to the beach. We went swimming in the sea.
MAN: Was the water cold?
BOY: No, it was warm.
3
BOY: We went to the beach again on Saturday.
MAN: Oh, that's nice.
BOY: Yes, but the water was colder so we played tennis instead.
MAN: Do you play tennis well?
BOY: Yes, but my parents played badly so we laughed a lot.
4
MAN: Did you fly your new kite?
BOY: Yes, on Monday it was windy.
MAN: Did you fly it on the beach?
BOY: No, I went to the park with my friends.
5
BOY: One day I went climbing with my mum.
MAN: Which day was that? Sunday?
BOY: No, Thursday, I think … Yes, it was.
MAN: Do you like climbing?
BOY: Yes, it's a bit difficult but it's very exciting.

HEADING: *Now listen again.*
(The tapescript is repeated.)

Pages 4 and 5: Listening Part 4 (5 marks)

Key: I A, 2 C, 3 C, 4 B, 5 A.

TRACK 23

HEADING: *Look at the pictures. Listen and look. There is one example.*
What was the matter with Jim?
WOMAN: Hello, Jim. Why didn't you go to school yesterday?
BOY: I was ill.
WOMAN: Oh dear. Did you have a stomach-ache?
BOY: No, I had a temperature.
WOMAN: Was that because you had a headache?
BOY: No, but I had a very bad earache.

HEADING: *Can you see the tick? Now you listen and tick the box.*
I Which is the doctor?
WOMAN: Do you feel better now?
BOY: Yes, because I went to the doctor and she gave me some medicine.
WOMAN: Who's your doctor?
BOY: Doctor Fine.
WOMAN: Is she the one with glasses and long hair?
BOY: She wears glasses but she has short hair.
WOMAN: Oh, yes. I know who she is.
2 Where did Jim go on Friday?
BOY: I think I got the earache on Friday because it was very windy.
WOMAN: Did you go to the park?
BOY: No, I went sailing with my dad.
WOMAN: In the lake?
BOY: No, we went sailing in the sea.
3 What does Jim like best?
WOMAN: Do you like sailing?
BOY: Yes, but I like skating best.
WOMAN: Do you skate in the park?
BOY: Yes, I always go with my friends. It's great.
4 How old is Jim's sister?
WOMAN: Did you go skating with your friends on Saturday?
BOY: No, it was my sister's birthday so she had a party.
WOMAN: Is your sister older or younger than you?
BOY: She's younger than me. I'm ten and she's eight.
WOMAN: And where was the party?
BOY: At home. My grandparents came with my aunt, my uncle and my cousins. There were eleven of us!
5 How many books did she have for her birthday?
WOMAN: Did you give your sister a present?
BOY: Yes, a book.
WOMAN: Does she like reading?
BOY: Yes, she does. She had lots of books for her birthday.
WOMAN: How many?
BOY: Well, Mum and Dad gave her four and I gave her one, so that's five … oh, and three friends gave her books, too.
WOMAN: So she had eight books for her birthday!
BOY: That's right.

HEADING: *Now listen again.*
(The tapescript is repeated.)

Page 6: Listening Part 5 (5 marks)

Key: 1 Colour the cap of the man with a bad leg – purple.
2 Write DOCTOR on the door above the words Mary Jones.
3 Colour the door – green.
4 Colour the boy's truck – yellow.
5 Colour the jumper of the girl with glasses – red.

TRACK 24

HEADING: *Look at the picture. Listen and look.*
There is one example.
MAN: Can you see the doctor?
GIRL: Yes, I can. She's the woman who's standing by the door.
MAN: That's right. Look at her hair.
GIRL: Yes, it's very long!
MAN: That's right. Colour her hair black.
GIRL: OK.

HEADING: *Can you see the woman with long, black hair?*
This is an example. Now you listen and colour and write.
1
MAN: There's a man with a bad leg.
GIRL: Yes, a man next to the window.
MAN: Can you see his cap?
GIRL: Yes. Can I colour it purple?
MAN: Of course.
2
MAN: Do you want to write a word for me?
GIRL: Yes, please.
MAN: Can you see the words MARY JONES on the door?
GIRL: Yes. Is that the doctor's name?
MAN: That's right. Can you write the word DOCTOR above
   her name?
GIRL: OK. I'm writing DOCTOR now.
3
GIRL: Can I colour the door?
MAN: Of course. What colour do you want to use?
GIRL: I'd like to use green.
MAN: That's a nice colour for a door.
4
MAN: Now, can you see the boy with stomach-ache?
GIRL: Which one?
MAN: The one with a truck.
GIRL: Yes, I can see him. Can I colour the truck?
MAN: Yes. You can choose the colour.
GIRL: OK. I'm doing it yellow.
5
GIRL: OK. What now?
MAN: Can you see the girl?
GIRL: There are two in the picture.
MAN: You're right. Look at the one who's wearing glasses.
   Colour her jumper red.
GIRL: OK. I like the picture now.
MAN: Yes, it's nice.

HEADING: *Now listen again.*
(The tapescript is repeated.)

Pages 7 and 8: Reading & Writing Part 1 (6 marks)

Key: 1 glasses, 2 a moustache, 3 a ruler, 4 a boat, 5 a bat,
   6 a doctor.

Pages 9 and 10: Reading & Writing Part 2 (6 marks)

Key: 1 no, 2 yes, 3 yes, 4 no, 5 yes, 6 no.

Pages 11 and 12: Reading & Writing Part 3 (6 marks)

Key: 1 A, 2 B, 3 A, 4 C, 5 B, 6 C.

Pages 13 and 14: Reading & Writing Part 4 (7 marks)

Key: 1 tennis, 2 girl, 3 ball, 4 ran, 5 happy, 6 day,
   7 The baseball game.

Pages 15, 16 and 17: Reading & Writing Part 5 (10 marks)

Key: 1 in the city, 2 Science//science, 3 Mary//His sister,
4 the human body, 5 home, 6 interesting, 7 need oxygen,
8 balloons//a balloon, 9 measured, 10 Science//science.

Pages 18 and 19: Reading & Writing Part 6 (5 marks)

Key: 1 are, 2 by, 3 their, 4 after, 5 first.

Pages 20, 21 and 22: Speaking (20 marks)

PREPARATION
- Photocopy, colour and cut out the cards on pages 110–112.
- Mount them on card and laminate them, if possible, for future use.
- Prepare Reinforcement or Extension worksheets or other work for the rest of the class to do while you work with individual pupils on the Speaking test.

Procedure
- Ask the pupil how old he/she is.
- Ask the pupil to describe several differences between the two pictures shown on the Find the Differences card,
  e.g. *This boy is going slowly, but this boy is going quickly.*
- Begin to tell the story prompted by the Picture Story card, e.g. *John is going out. His mum says he must wear his coat. He doesn't want to wear it.* Ask the pupil to continue with the story.
- Ask the pupil to choose one picture in each set of four on the Odd-One-Out card, and explain why it is the odd one out in the set, e.g. *These are all people, but this is a chair.*
- Ask questions about the pupil, e.g. *What weather do you like?*

Page 1: Listening Part 1 (5 marks)

Key: Lines should be drawn between:
1 Anna and the girl by the window
2 May and the taller woman standing by the map
3 Kim and the girl standing by the boat taking photos
4 Daisy and the girl standing in front of the picture of the sea
5 John and the man sitting down with a jacket on

TRACK 25

HEADING: *Look at the picture. Listen and look. There is one example.*
WOMAN: Hello, Tom. What are you doing here?
BOY: We're visiting the museum.
WOMAN: Are you here with the school?
BOY: No, I'm with my aunt and uncle and my cousins.
WOMAN: Who's that by the door?
BOY: The boy wearing a cap?
WOMAN: Yes.
BOY: That's Fred.

HEADING: *Can you see the line? This is an example. Now you listen and draw lines.*
1
WOMAN: Who's the girl by the window?
BOY: By the window, with curly hair?
WOMAN: Yes, that's right.
BOY: That's my cousin, Anna.
2
WOMAN: That's a nice map, isn't it?
BOY: Yes, it is and it's very interesting.
WOMAN: Who's the taller woman standing by it?
BOY: The taller one?
WOMAN: Yes.
BOY: That's my Aunt May.
3
WOMAN: I like that boat.
BOY: So does Kim. Look! She's taking a photo of it.
WOMAN: Oh, is that Kim?
BOY: Yes. She loves her camera!
4
WOMAN: I can't see that picture near the door very well.
BOY: I think it's a picture of the sea, but we can ask Daisy because she is standing in front of it now.
5
WOMAN: Is that man your uncle?
BOY: No, not that man. My Uncle John is the man sitting down.
WOMAN: The one with the jacket on?
BOY: That's right.

HEADING: *Now listen again.*
(The tapescript is repeated.)

Page 2: Listening Part 2 (5 marks)

Key: 1 ten//10, 2 eleven//11, 3 cake, 4 three//3, 5 Clouds.

TRACK 26

HEADING: *Listen and look. There is one example.*
MAN: What are you doing, John?
BOY: I'm buying food and drink for my birthday party.
MAN: When is the party?
BOY: On Friday.
MAN: This Friday?
BOY: Yes, that's right.

HEADING: *Can you see the answer? Now you listen and write.*
1
MAN: Are you inviting a lot of children to your party?
BOY: Yes, ten of my friends are coming.
MAN: Ten? That's nice!
2
MAN: Are all your friends the same age as you?
BOY: Most are but Mary is twelve.
MAN: And are you eleven?
BOY: Yes, I'm eleven on Friday.
3
MAN: What food are you buying?
BOY: Sausages, hamburgers, crisps, bread and cake.
MAN: What's your favourite food?
BOY: Cake.
4
MAN: Are those drinks for the party, too?
BOY: Yes, there's juice and water.
MAN: How many bottles?
BOY: Two of juice and three of water.
MAN: Did you say three bottles of water?
BOY: Yes, that's right.
5
MAN: Are you having the party at home?
BOY: Yes, I am, but we want to see a film at the cinema after the party.
MAN: What film?
BOY: It's called *Clouds*.
MAN: Clowns?
BOY: No! *Clouds*! C L O U D S!
MAN: Oh, sorry! Have a nice party!

HEADING: *Now listen again.*
(The tapescript is repeated.)

Page 3: Listening Part 3 (5 marks)

Key:

Friday	Monday
Thursday	Wednesday
Saturday (example)	Tuesday

TRACK 27

HEADING: *Look at the pictures. What did Sally do last week? Listen and look. There is one example.*

MAN: Hello, Sally. How are you?
GIRL: I'm fine, thanks.
MAN: I didn't see you on Saturday.
GIRL: No, I went to the zoo with my cousins.

HEADING: *Can you see the line from the word Saturday? On Saturday, Sally went to the zoo with her cousins. Now you listen and draw lines.*

1
MAN: Were your cousins with you all week?
GIRL: No, they left on Monday evening but that day, in the morning, we went to the Natural History Museum.
MAN: Was that interesting?
GIRL: Yes, I learnt a lot.

2
MAN: Do your cousins visit you every weekend?
GIRL: No, but on Friday I emailed them to invite them to my house.
MAN: Did you email them from the library?
GIRL: No, I have a computer in my room.
MAN: You're lucky.
GIRL: I know!

3
MAN: Which was your best day last week?
GIRL: Tuesday.
MAN: Why's that?
GIRL: Because it was my birthday and I had a party.
MAN: How old were you?
GIRL: Ten.

4
GIRL: On Wednesday, I went to the shops because I had to buy some clothes.
MAN: It rained then, didn't it?
GIRL: Yes, that's why we had to go by car.

5
MAN: But it didn't rain every day last week.
GIRL: No, on Thursday, it was very sunny. We went to the shops again but we went by bike.
MAN: I see.

HEADING: *Now listen again.*
(The tapescript is repeated.)

Pages 4 and 5: Listening Part 4 (5 marks)

Key: 1 C, 2 A, 3 B, 4 C, 5 A.

TRACK 28

HEADING: *Look at the pictures. Listen and look. There is one example.*

Where did Jack go?
WOMAN: Did you go swimming yesterday?
BOY: No, I don't go swimming on Tuesdays.
WOMAN: What did you do?
BOY: I went to the shops.
WOMAN: With your friends?
BOY: No, I went with my parents and my sister, Jane.

HEADING: *Can you see the tick? Now you listen and tick the box.*

1 What did Jack's parents buy him?
WOMAN: Did you buy anything?
BOY: Yes, we all bought something. My mum bought a DVD and my dad bought a new mouse, but the best thing was that they bought me a camera.

2 What did their parents buy for Jack's sister?
WOMAN: What about Jane? Did your parents buy her a camera, too?
BOY: No, she takes photos on her mobile phone. They bought her an MP3 player.
WOMAN: And a new computer?
BOY: No!

3 What animals did Jack take photos of?
WOMAN: Did you use your camera?
BOY: Yes, because when we finished shopping, we went to the zoo.
WOMAN: Did you take photos of the giraffes?
BOY: There weren't any giraffes but I took a lot of photos of the dolphins.
WOMAN: Ah! What about the snakes?
BOY: Urgh, yuck, no!

4 What did they eat at the zoo?
WOMAN: Did you have a snack at the zoo?
BOY: We wanted to take a picnic but we thought it could rain so we went to the café.
WOMAN: Did you eat burgers or sandwiches?
BOY: Sandwiches.

5 What toy animal did Jack buy?
WOMAN: Did you go to the zoo shop?
BOY: Yes. There were lots of toys. I liked the toy animals.
WOMAN: Did you buy one?
BOY: Yes, but it was difficult to decide. I liked the elephants and the monkeys but then I saw a panda and I liked that most.
WOMAN: So, did you buy the panda?
BOY: Yes. Look, I've got it here.
WOMAN: Oh!

HEADING: *Now listen again.*
(The tapescript is repeated.)

Page 6: Listening Part 5 (5 marks)

Key: 1 Draw a cat in the blank frame.
2 Colour the woman's bag – red.
3 Colour the man's book – blue.
4 Colour the picture of the car – yellow.
5 Colour the flowers in the picture – orange.

TRACK 29

HEADING: *Look at the picture. Listen and look. There is one example.*
MAN: Can you see the girl?
GIRL: Which one? I can see three girls.
MAN: You're right. The tallest one.
GIRL: Yes.
MAN: Can you colour her shoes black?
GIRL: OK.

HEADING: *Can you see the girl with black shoes? This is an example. Now you listen and colour and draw.*
1
GIRL: I'd like to draw something.
MAN: OK. The tallest girl is looking at a picture of a cat.
GIRL: I can't see a cat!
MAN: No, but you can draw it!
GIRL: OK. I'm drawing a cat.
2
GIRL: Now I'd like to colour something.
MAN: All right. Can you see the woman carrying a bag?
GIRL: Yes. Can I colour her bag?
MAN: Yes, I think red would be nice.
GIRL: So do I.
3
MAN: Can you see the man sitting down?
GIRL: Yes. He's got a book.
MAN: That's right.
GIRL: Can I colour the book?
MAN: Yes, good idea!
GIRL: What colour?
MAN: Er … blue.
4
GIRL: There's a nice picture of a car.
MAN: You're right. It looks like a fast car.
GIRL: Yes. Can I colour it yellow?
MAN: OK. That's a good colour.
5
GIRL: My favourite painting is the one of the flowers.
MAN: Yes, they are beautiful!
GIRL: Can I colour the flowers?
MAN: Of course. I think orange would be nice.
GIRL: So do I.

HEADING: *Now listen again.*
(The tapescript is repeated.)

Pages 7 and 8: Reading & Writing Part 1 (6 marks)

Key: 1 a map, 2 a forest, 3 a giraffe, 4 a button, 5 a pen, 6 a camera.

Pages 9 and 10: Reading & Writing Part 2 (6 marks)

Key: 1 yes, 2 no, 3 no, 4 yes, 5 no, 6 yes.

Pages 11 and 12: Reading & Writing Part 3 (6 marks)

Key: 1 B, 2 C, 3 A, 4 B, 5 A, 6 C.

Pages 13 and 14: Reading & Writing Part 4 (7 marks)

Key: 1 morning, 2 presents, 3 six, 4 living room, 5 shouted, 6 food, 7 Dad's party.

Pages 15, 16 and 17: Reading & Writing Part 5 (10 marks)

Key: 1 stories, 2 read, 3 the/a piano, 4 it was sunny, 5 taller, 6 the funniest, 7 after, 8 black and white, 9 drinking water, 10 than.

Pages 18 and 19: Reading & Writing Part 6 (5 marks)

Key: 1 in, 2 eat, 3 every, 4 are, 5 can.

Pages 20, 21 and 22: Speaking (20 marks)

Preparation
● Photocopy, colour and cut out the cards on pages 133–135.
● Mount them on card and laminate them, if possible, for future use.
● Prepare Reinforcement or Extension worksheets or other work for the rest of the class to do while you work with individual pupils on the Speaking test.

Procedure
● Ask the pupil how old he/she is.
● Ask the pupil to describe several differences between the two pictures shown on the Find the Differences card, e.g. *This boy is sitting down, but this boy is standing up.*
● Begin to tell the story prompted by the Picture Story card, e.g. *It's a sunny day. Peter's grandad is sleeping in the garden. Peter goes out of the garden. The duck goes after him.* Ask the pupil to continue with the story.
● Ask the pupil to choose one picture in each set of four on the Odd-One-Out card, and explain why it is the odd one out in the set, e.g. *These three are food but this is a bowl.*
● Ask questions about the pupil, e.g. *Can you play an instrument?*

Name cards

Alex	Jack	Mary	Sally
Ann	Jane	May	Sam
Anna	Jill	Nick	Sue
Ben	Jim	Pat	Tom
Bill	John	Paul	Tony
Daisy	Kim	Peter	Vicky
Fred	Lucy		

Kid's Box Teacher's Resource Book 4 Name cards   © Cambridge University Press 2015   PHOTOCOPIABLE

Diploma

This is to certify that

....

....

has completed

Level 4 of KID'S BOX

School ....

Teacher ....

Date ....

Thanks and acknowledgements

The authors would like to express their warmest thanks to Pippa Mayfield for her impeccable editing and great sense of fun throughout the project.

Kathryn Escribano would like to thank the staff and children at the CP Narciso Alonso Cortés, Valladolid (Spain) on whom the ideas have been tried and tested. She would also like to acknowledge the patience and understanding of her family and friends from whom time was taken to write this book.

The authors and publishers are grateful to the following illustrators:

Adrian Barclay, c/o Beehive; Julian Mosedale; Lisa Smith, c/o Sylvie Poggio; Gwyneth Williamson; Kelly Kennedy, c/o Sylvie Poggio

The publishers are grateful to the following contributors:

Pentacorbig: concept design, cover design, book design and page make-up
Wild Apple Design: second edition cover design and page make-up
John Green and Tim Woolf, TEFL Audio: audio recordings
Songs written and produced by Robert Lee, Dib Dib Dub Studios

Track listing